What Your Colleagues Are S

MW00806990

Sugata Mitra is one of the most original voices in education today. His unique research with children and technology around the world casts a fascinating light on the core dynamics of learning—and teaching. Children love to learn; they don't all do well in education. Why not? In school they're usually obliged to compete with each other; what if they collaborate instead? They're typically taught by age; what happens when they're not? What if there's no teacher at all? And what does all of this mean for the future of education in an increasingly connected and febrile world? A bold, provocative, and important book for anyone with a serious interest in learning, technology, and schools.

—Sir Ken Robinson, PhD
Educator and *New York Times* Best-Selling Author

We universally underestimate children. Sugata Mitra does not. His life's work has been to enable children to explore for themselves, using their innate curiosity and imagination. Education is what people do to you. Learning is what you do to yourself. Digital ether allows that latter, as you will see in this book.

—Nicholas Negroponte
Founder, MIT Media Lab and One Laptop per Child

Sugata Mitra's new book is arresting. It stops you in your tracks and causes you to think again. Many a good book will encourage and guide; and some will recommend better ways of doing things. This book does all of that and more. It also questions popular convention and provokes you into a new way of thinking about learning.

For example, think of the millions spent on providing enough computers for every student, or at least one device between two students; whereas Sugata Mitra shows that children will learn at greater rates if they cluster around large screens, in mixed-age groups, and discover together. Or, think of the ways in which ICT teaching carefully plans a step-by-step approach to ensure the "right" thing is studied at the right time, whereas Mitra shows children who are given free and public access to computers and the internet can become computer literate without the need for a planned curriculum. Perhaps most profound of all, Mitra describes the conditions leading to a self-organized learning environment (SOLE) in which, contrary to the usual situation in which students cram for a test and then forget much of what they've learned once the test is done, the students in his experiments actually knew *more* when they were given a surprise test months later! As for the School in the Cloud idea, the underlying principle is to *not* "teach"; instead, have a conversation, raise questions, and ask children to work out possible answers—but do not "teach"!

On reading this book I suspect, like me, you will think the following quote will prove prophetic when considering Sugata Mitra's contribution to education; I just hope that by reading and acting upon the messages herein, we can hasten toward that celebration: in the words of Nicholas Klein, "First they ignore you. Then they ridicule you. And then they attack you and want to burn you. And then they build monuments to you."

—James Nottingham, Founder and Author
The Learning Challenge
Challenging Learning
Alnmouth, UK

Sugata Mitra's long-awaited book is not only a documentation of two decades of studies into self-organized learning, it is also an invitation to explore the mind of a disruptor. Mitra deftly traces the history of his projects, offering keen insights into the thinking behind his celebrated Hole-in-the-Wall and Schools-in-the-Cloud experiments. He provides a compelling, personal, and at times contentious narrative, replete with evidence that when given the right conditions, children really can learn for themselves. For educators everywhere, *The School in the Cloud* will be challenging and inspirational in equal measure.

—Steve Wheeler
Learning Innovation Consultant
Former Associate Professor of Education
Plymouth Institute of Education

Sugata Mitra is the standard-bearer for a genuinely 21st century education—one that connects children's innate thirst and capacity for learning with the massive resource of the internet, and then gets out of the way and lets them run free and grow their minds in the process. Read this book and let your sense of what is possible for children to do and become be expanded beyond your wildest dreams. And join Mitra's crusading army of angels—for his radical yet practical ideas are opposed by many who have done well by systematically underestimating children's capabilities.

—Guy Claxton
Author, *The Learning Power Approach: Teaching Learners to Teach Themselves*

The internet provides a seemingly endless resource beyond just consumption. Leveraging years of research, Sugata Mitra provides a compelling narrative on how the internet can empower kids to learn in ways we never imagined. The wisdom and strategies he shares serve as a blueprint to transform education now and in the future.

—Eric Sheninger
Senior Fellow and Thought Leader on Digital Leadership
International Center for Leadership in Education (ICLE)

Many people profess to know what the future of school will be. These claims are often vague, overconfident, or overly simplistic. Not here. This book is filled with examples, questions, humility, possibilities, and undeniable stories that should make us all uncomfortable with our current ways of thinking about education. This is a must-read for all who want to expand their understanding about learning.

—Julie Stern
Author, *Tools for Teaching Conceptual Understanding*

Twenty years ago, Sugata Mitra disrupted traditional education by installing a computer kiosk in an Indian slum and inviting children to learn together—without teachers, textbooks, or tests. Lessons from that first Hole-in-the-Wall experiment have informed the global development of what Mitra calls self-organized learning environments (or SOLEs), where children investigate "big questions" by conducting online research. In *The School in the Cloud*, Mitra doesn't call for the end of schools or the elimination of teachers. Rather, he shows what's possible when educators embrace the SOLE model. With data and storytelling, he paints a picture of education that's sparked by curiosity, enabled by technology, and facilitated by teachers who are wise enough to let children drive their own learning.

—Suzie Boss
Writer and Educational Consultant
Co-author, *Thinking Through Project-Based Learning*
Portland, OR

In *The School in the Cloud*, Sugata Mitra presents learning at its most elemental—a child's need to know combines with open access to information and gentle encouragement and her or his potential as a learner takes off. Readers familiar with high-quality project-based learning (PBL) will appreciate that Mitra's work gets at the essence of this methodology. And, in its way, his book is the embodiment of the very processes Mitra recommends. In this book, we follow Mitra as he identifies an urgent concern (poor access to education), investigates and tries to address it, and through iteration and improvement, settles on a solution. We're lucky he shares it with others. With humor, humility, and insights borne from both successes and setbacks, Mitra shares lessons that, at their germ, show how student-centered, inquiry-driven learning can take shape, no matter the context.

—Jane Krauss
Curriculum and Program Development Consultant
National Center for Women & Information Technology
Co-author, *Thinking Through Project-Based Learning*
Eugene, OR

For many years Sugata Mitra has been one of very few saying, and evidencing, that we should properly trust children with their learning. Children saw right away that they needed to know about the past to imagine and then build their futures. So of course they know how important it is to practice imagining. Children don't need this book; this book is for everyone else.

—Stephen Heppell
Professor and Felipe Segovia Chair in Learning Innovation
Universidad Camilo José Cela, Madrid

This book is dedicated to
The Gupinath of Dasghara
Who read it before it was written.

THE SCHOOL
IN THE
CLOUD

THE
EMERGING
FUTURE
OF LEARNING

• • •

SUGATA
MITRA

FOREWORDS BY JOHN HATTIE AND
CLASS 3G, BELLEVILLE PRIMARY SCHOOL

CORWIN

FOR INFORMATION:

Corwin

A SAGE Company

2455 Teller Road

Thousand Oaks, California 91320

(800) 233-9936

www.corwin.com

SAGE Publications Ltd.

1 Oliver's Yard

55 City Road

London EC1Y 1SP

United Kingdom

SAGE Publications India Pvt. Ltd.

B 1/I 1 Mohan Cooperative Industrial Area

Mathura Road, New Delhi 110 044

India

SAGE Publications Asia-Pacific Pte. Ltd.

18 Cross Street #10-10/11/12

China Square Central

Singapore 048423

Acquisitions Editor: Ariel Curry

Development Editor: Desirée A. Bartlett

Associate Content

Development Editor: Jessica Vidal

Project Editor: Amy Schroller

Copy Editor: Karen E. Taylor

Typesetter: C&M Digitals (P) Ltd.

Proofreader: Rae-Ann Goodwin

Indexer: Sheila Bodell

Cover Designer: Janet Kiesel

Marketing Manager: Margaret O'Connor

Printed in the United States of America

ISBN 978-1-5063-8917-2

This book is printed on acid-free paper.

19 20 21 22 23 10 9 8 7 6 5 4 3 2 1

DISCLAIMER: This book may direct you to access third-party content via Web links, QR codes, or other scannable technologies, which are provided for your reference by the author(s). Corwin makes no guarantee that such third-party content will be available for your use and encourages you to review the terms and conditions of such third-party content. Corwin takes no responsibility and assumes no liability for your use of any third-party content, nor does Corwin approve, sponsor, endorse, verify, or certify such third-party content.

CONTENTS

PART II: SCHOOLS IN THE CLOUD

PART III: GLIMPSES OF THE FUTURE OF LEARNING

Visit the companion website at
http://resources.corwin.com/schoolinthecloud
for videos and additional resources.

LIST OF FIGURES

LIST OF COMPANION WEBSITE RESOURCES

Note From the Publisher: The author has provided video and web content throughout the book that is available to you through QR (quick response) codes. To read a QR code, you must have a smartphone or tablet with a camera. We recommend that you download a QR code reader app that is made specifically for your phone or tablet brand.

Videos and resources may also be accessed at **http://resources.corwin.com/school inthecloud.**

Introduction

Video 0.1 Edge of Chaos

Chapter 1

Link 1.1 The Granny Cloud: www.thegrannycloud.org

Video 1.1 Krishanu

Video 1.2 *Gateshead Granny Cloud*

Chapter 2

Video 2.1 *Kids Can Teach Themselves*

Video 2.2 *The Child-Driven Education*

Video 2.3 *Build a School in the Cloud*

Chapter 4

Video 4.1 Korakati

Chapter 5

Video 5.1 Chandrakona

References

FOREWORD

Put a dot on a piece of paper, make some simple rules, and from this you have a whole new education model that truly makes the difference to children in any situation. If you think it's not possible, then you need to open your mind before you read this book. Rather than re-create what we know about schooling to adapt to the Indian slums and indeed to all schooling, we need to think again, starting with a simple idea—a dot—and working forward from it. This remarkable journey of a dot to an innovation about the School in the Cloud could apply anywhere in the world, for rich and poor, but it needs an open mind and a sense of wonder.

In the Western world, there is a grammar of schooling (Tyack & Cuban, 1995; Tyack & Tobin, 1994): one teacher talking and talking; 20–30+ students, clustered by age; self-contained classrooms; textbooks; testing; and grades. There is also a grammar of learning with facts, knowledge, and surface ideas being privileged and lots of doing and hoping thence for learning, a focus on interesting and engaging activities to keep students busy—and rarely is there teaching of alternative strategies such that if students do not learn they can have backup strategies. As Jenkins (2008) shows, while 97 percent or more of 5-year-olds want to come to school to learn, this drops to 30–40 percent at the end of elementary school, and slightly rises in high school—meaning about five to seven high school students per class come to school wanting to learn. Despite this, Western schools have performed well on national and international tests (which favor "knowing lots"), and there is much evidence that many teachers develop deeper learning, foster curiosity, and make classes inviting places for students to want to come and learn (Hattie, 2009). This model is expensive not only in dollars but also in the development of the needed expertise of teachers and school leaders to run these schools. So what chance do students have in countries without these resources and this long history of providing school systems? Can we wait until we build these schools before we improve the achievements of these students?

Along comes Sugata Mitra who asks not how to replicate the successes (or otherwise) of the Western world but how we can use the technologies that are now available to conceive of a totally different type of schooling. He started with an idea, moved to a "Hole in the Wall," and now to the School in the Cloud. He had a vision for what this hole and cloud would achieve: It was not "let's hope and see what happens"—it was a deliberate move to teach both the facts and knowledge needed to then problem solve, create, and relate ideas. There was no mission to make students "know lots"; they were to know enough to then relate, extend, discover, and create. This balance was so important to the vision.

Recently, we synthesized many learning strategies trying to ascertain which were most effective, when, and why (Hattie & Donoghue, 2016). We found that some strategies worked effectively toward certain ends: they enabled people either to learn the bits of knowledge but not the relations between those bits knowledge—or vice versa. This balance of surface and deep knowing is core—and we noted that so many (almost all) teaching methods were either effective for surface or for deep learning. An exception was the "jigsaw method" whereby a teacher introduces a main topic and several subtopics. Students are broken into home groups, and each member of the home group is assigned a subtopic. Then, students form expert groups to study their assigned subtopic through research and discussion. After the students have mastered the subtopic in question, they return to their home group to report on their findings. At the conclusion of the exercise, each home group member has learned about each subtopic from a member of the relevant expert group or through her or his own investigation with an expert group. Often the "jigsaw" concludes with a unifying activity or task. The power comes from balancing the surface and deep learning, ensuring students have the knowledge before asking them to use this knowledge, and making every student responsible, a learner and a key part in the learning of the whole group.

How different is this from providing students with access to the internet (to gain the surface knowledge) and then asking them to engage in tasks that use this knowledge? (Many Western teachers who overemphasize knowing lots might flinch to hear they would be replaced by the internet in this scenario!) The internet teaches students language and questioning and search methods, and it demands that they learn to distinguish between opinions, indoctrination, and propaganda. At the same time, it offers students access over these computers to "English Grannies" who read them stories (not teaching, just stories); the students hear the English, enjoy the stories, and become engaged in conversations with the Grannies. With these skills, children are more than ready to move from knowledge, to topics, to problems. To be curious, to explore, to see relations between ideas, to want to know more—this is what we want for all our students.

The "Visible Learning" messages resonate throughout this book, starting with getting the right balance between the surface and the deep aspects of knowing. The students are asked to evaluate their learning continually, to develop high expectations about what they can learn, and to focus on what they are going to learn and not what they are going to do, to use the Goldilocks principles of challenge—not too hard, not too boring (note the excellent six levels of cognitive complexity in Chapter 2). They are encouraged to welcome errors and misconceptions as opportunities to learn and to maximize opportunities to seek and receive feedback about where to venture next in their learning. These strategies all maximize the chance of learning, put the power of learning into the students' hands, and, most of all, epitomize the aim to "make students see themselves as their own teachers."

There is no shying away from evidence about the effectiveness of this model—and a major theme is asking how we should measure students' learning and depth of understanding. Where should we go next? How can we draw out learning to create new, stimulating, open, and engaging questions for subsequent sessions? And how can we prevent boredom and engage in appropriately challenging learning?

While many of the messages seem to relate to India and places with fewer resources, there are many examples of the School in the Cloud working everywhere. But it will require a transfer of power and centrality—teachers will have to learn to talk less, to accept the internet as a primary resource ("on the internet you know before you learn"), to evaluate learning in terms of both knowing lots *and* understanding deeply, to give up much of the current crowded curriculum, to get used to moving bodies in the school and not fixed classrooms, and to appreciate the vast reservoir of untapped excitement and potential that every student can use if not constrained to straight rows, bells, teacher talk, and too much doing.

Recall the story of the learned professor who went to a School in the Cloud and during the sessions was amazed and impressed—but, at the end of the day, proclaimed, "Now I need to go back to my office to see if this will work in theory." Yes, there is a lot to do, but this book screams success, breaks artificial ceilings of low expectations, and shows that what works brilliantly for poor students can also work for rich students (so often what works in rich nations may not work in poor nations).

Sugata is a person with a dangerous idea—and it just might work. He powerfully joins the dots. Enjoy the thrill of being on the edge with him, because at the edge of chaos anything might happen.

—John Hattie
Graduate School of Education
University of Melbourne, Australia

FOREWORD

Written collectively by the pupils of Class 3G, Belleville Primary School, London, England

Sugata Mitra's Notes

Can children write a foreword to a book about children's learning? To test this, I went to Belleville Primary School in London, England. Belleville Primary is a part of the Quality First Education Trust. The principal of the school, John Grove, had invited me years ago to visit his school and demonstrate SOLEs (self-organized learning environments, about which you will read in this book). Since that time, I have visited his school many times and conducted some really interesting sessions with children. This time, it was with a research question—Is there something called "collective writing," an expression of the "collective voice"?

The experiment was done with 7-year-olds of class 3G. I met the children and explained that I had written a book, and I would like them to write a foreword for that book, one that was from them. They did not know what a foreword was. "You figure the rest out," I told them.

A group of teachers watched the process as observers and facilitated access to the resources needed for the experiment. I had instructed them not to speak to the children at all. The group of observing teachers formed my research group for later discussions. They were Andrew Furniss, Karen Taylor, and Alexandra Edwards led by Tom Greene and James Canniford. They, along with Principal John Grove, made this experiment possible, and I am grateful to them.

Taking printouts of the seven key chapters of this book, The School in the Cloud: The Emerging Future of Learning, the children distributed themselves into fluid groups of approximately four. In the next few minutes, each group elected a reader, who read the chapter aloud; a researcher, who searched the internet for words and ideas they did not understand; and two scribes, who made notes about all this. Amazingly, all this happened by itself.

I returned to the school about ten days later to find that the children had figured out what a foreword was and, using their notes from the first day, had constructed a collective document.

Here is that amazing piece of work. It has not been edited.

This book is about pupils learning in a self-organised learning environment (SOLE). In countries all over the world young people have been doing SOLEs. SOLE is about children being in charge of their own learning. When they work together in a SOLE they don't use teachers. Children need no more teachers because they should have more SOLE lessons. This isn't another ordinary book about teachers. It's a book about how students can work independently and teach themselves. It also contains information on how children can be in charge of their own learning. SOLE is something Sugata Mitra wants to do more.

The problems with teaching are that in all of the lessons we have been in teachers gave us clues or answers on the subject. Children answer the questions. The problem with teaching is that sometimes the teacher gets tired out. If you let the children do SOLE, it's like the problem never existed. Teaching is telling, so we would like to use more independent work. Students need their independence. Pupils need power.

This book aims to fix those problems by children learning by themselves. They can talk in groups so they learn from others.

We think that you will notice a strong emphasis in this book on children being in charge of their own learning. Children have been working by themselves for several years because of SOLE lessons. Kids have been learning with adults but Professor Mitra has changed this system. Children are independent and they do SOLE lessons in groups.

Children have been learning with teachers but Professor Mitra changed that and made pupils learn by themselves so they are independent enough. You'll also notice a strong emphasis on students being in charge of their own learning and don't need teachers to help them. Young learners have been working by themselves for years now because of SOLE.

This book is particularly important because it shows how children can develop their learning independently. Flick through these pages and see how important children's access to the internet is. You'll find out that Sugata Mitra supports pupils learning independently or in groups.

This book is about children but is for adults. Children should be able to educate alone independently. Pupils can learn by themselves. You will be reading this book because it is about SOLE. This isn't another book about boring old teachers, it is to help see your child doesn't need a teacher. We think students can learn in the 'cloud'. You will enjoy this book because Professor Mitra is a very experienced teacher. As you run through the book imagine what you could do as a learning method.

—Class 3G
Belleville Primary School
Clapham, London

ACKNOWLEDGMENTS

This book is the work of children. I am just their messenger. When I first started my experiments in 1999 and was asked to present and publish, I was very worried because I had no formal understanding of social science. I knew a bit of physics; I knew how to speak about and publish things about physics.

So I decided that if I had to "do" social science, I would stick to two statements—"this is what I did" and "this is what I observed." If I lived those two sentences honestly and to the best of my abilities, I would be safe. This book follows those sentences as far as possible. I have avoided opinions, others' or mine. There is no "this is what I think" or "this is what someone told me" in this book. By and large!

There are many people who helped me to do the work reported in this book and many who helped me write it. If I try to list them, the list will be incomplete and unfair.

There are organizations that funded the work done in all these years. They are easier to list. Rajendra Pawar and Vijay Thadani, then chairperson and CEO, respectively, of NIIT Limited in India, tolerated my idiosyncrasies for close to 20 years. Mrs. Aruna Asaf Ali, chairperson and legend, insisted on calling me "our computer" when I was working at the *Patriot* newspaper. Sheila Dixit, then chief minister of Delhi, loved the Hole-in-the-Wall experiments and told me not to put on weight while doing them. The social responsibility wing of the ICICI Bank in India funded me against stiff resistance from "up there." James Wofensohn, then president of the World Bank, asked, "How much do you need?" James Tooley brought me to England. Newcastle University of England employed me and never asked where I was and when I would return. Nicholas Negroponte of MIT Media Lab warned me not to mess with things I didn't understand. And Chris Anderson of TED paid me the best compliment I have ever received: "I think he knows what he is doing," he said. And then he put me on the TED stage without rehearsal and gave me a million dollars. These people helped me do my work—they need the full credit for all that happened.

And then there are teachers all around the world—a better lot of people you would be hard put to find. They were always kind while pointing out the mistakes I was making.

And finally, all my friends, those jolly good folks, in spite of whom this book got written.

PUBLISHER'S ACKNOWLEDGMENTS

Corwin gratefully acknowledges the contributions of the following:

Barbara Z. Boone, retired elementary teacher
Baltimore County Public School System
Towson, MD

Kelly Fitzgerald, Instructional Coach
Rouse High School
Leander, TX

ABOUT THE AUTHOR

Sugata Mitra's current work is on the internet and children's learning. He retired in 2019 as Professor of Educational Technology at Newcastle University in the UK and is currently an independent researcher, speaker, and author.

He conducted the Hole-in-the-Wall (HIW) experiment in 1999, embedding a computer within a wall in an Indian slum at Kalkaji, Delhi; children were allowed to use this computer freely. The experiment aimed at proving that kids could be taught computers very easily without any formal training. Mitra termed this minimally invasive education (MIE). The experiment has since been repeated at many places. He is the recipient of many awards and honorary doctorates from India, the United Kingdom, the United States, and many other countries in the world.

His interests include children's education, remote presence, self-organizing systems, cognitive systems, complex dynamical systems, physics, and consciousness.

The Hole-in-the-Wall experiment has left a mark on popular culture. Indian diplomat Vikas Swarup read about Mitra's experiment and was inspired to write his debut novel that went on to become the Oscar-winning movie of 2009—*Slumdog Millionaire*.

Mitra holds a PhD in physics and is credited with more that 25 inventions in the area of cognitive science and educational technology. He was conferred the prestigious Dewang Mehta Award for Innovation in Information Technology from the government of India in the year 2003. Among many other awards, he received the first ever million-dollar TED Prize in 2013.

Starting with molecular orbital computation in the 1970s, Mitra discovered that the structure of organic molecules determine their function more than the constituent atoms.

After a PhD in solid-state physics from the Indian Institute of Technology (IIT), Delhi, he went on to research energy storage systems, first at the Centre for

Energy Studies, IIT, and then at the Technische Universität, Vienna, Austria. This resulted in a new design for zinc-chlorine batteries.

His interests in the flow of electricity through biological systems, a consequence of his PhD research on exciton dissociation in organic semiconductors, led to a seminally speculative paper on why the human sense organs are located where they are.

His interest in computer networking led him toward the emerging systems in printing in the 1980s. He set up India's first local-area-network-based newspaper publishing system in 1984 and went on to predict the desktop publishing industry. This, in turn, led to the invention of LAN-based database publishing, and he created the "Yellow Pages" industry in India and Bangladesh.

His interest in the human mind once again led him into the areas of learning and memory, and he was among the first in the world to show that simulated neural networks can help decipher the mechanisms of Alzheimer's disease.

He was among the first people in the world to invent Voluntary Perception Recording (a continuously variable voting machine) and a hyperlinked computing environment in 1990, several years ahead of the World Wide Web.

Professor Mitra's work at NIIT created the first curricula and pedagogy for that organization; he followed by devoting years to research on learning styles, learning devices (several of them now patented), and multimedia and new methods of learning. Culminating and, perhaps, towering over his previous work are his "Hole-in-the-Wall" experiments with children's learning. Since 1999, he has convincingly demonstrated that groups of children, irrespective of who or where they are, can learn to use computers and the internet on their own using public computers in open spaces such as roads and playgrounds. He brought these results to England in 2006 and invented SOLEs (self-organized learning environments), now in use throughout the world. In 2009, he created the Granny Cloud of people who interact with children over the internet.

Since the 1970s, Professor Mitra's publications and work have resulted in the training and development of perhaps a million young Indians, among them some of the poorest children in the world.

Recently, he used the money he was awarded when he received the TED Prize to put his educational ideas together to create seven laboratories called "Schools in the Cloud." Here he studied learning as emergent phenomena in an educational self-organizing system. These results question the ideas of curriculum and examinations, as well as the meaning of "knowing" itself, in the internet world of the twenty-first century.

The effects of Sugata Mitra's work on the lives of people and the economies of the countries in which his "Schools in the Cloud" have existed can only be guessed at.

"

"My wish is to help design the future of learning by supporting children all over the world to tap into their innate sense of wonder. Help me build the School in the Cloud, a learning lab in India, where children can embark on intellectual adventures by engaging and connecting with information and mentoring online. I also invite you, wherever you are, to create your own miniature child-driven learning environments and share your discoveries."

Sugata Mitra
February 23, 2013, TED
Long Beach, California, USA

PRELUDE

A Matter of Imagination

Author's note

This prelude is about spontaneous order appearing in chaotic systems. Now, if that sounds a bit scary, I don't blame you. After all, you thought you were going to read a book about education. But believe me, there is a connection—a rather strange one. If you find this prelude distracting, skip it and go to Chapter 1. However, once you have read the whole book, may I request you to come back to this prelude? It might all make sense then . . . .

You can imagine anything. You could imagine a fish on fire inside a fish tank. What you imagine does not actually exist; it's just in your mind.

But what if the things you imagine do exist somewhere, in some reality? Could imagination then just be an organ, like your eyes? An organ that can see across many realities, across past, present, and future?

I ran into this idea while thinking about causality. Causality moves only from past to the present: the cause is always in the past, the effect in the present. Why should the cause always come *before* the effect? Could a cause come after the effect?

That sounded absurd, so I tried an experiment with my colleague Sujai. Many years ago now, we tried to build a time symmetric causal system—a system where things happen because of *both* what happened before and what will happen after. Sometimes, this is called "retrocausality." I like "time symmetric" better—the cause can exist before or after the effect.

The experiment was a simple computer program. We put a dot on a screen, and we made some simple rules for what will happen to the dot in the next instant. What happens to any dot on the screen depended on its neighbors on either side. For example, if a dot had one dot immediately to its left and right, it would be over-crowded and just disappear in the next instant. If a dot had no neighbors at all, it would be lonely and two dots would appear on either side of it. We made four such rules (of life and death, if you like!). So, the dots for each time step were computed using the dots of the previous time step.

These systems are called "cellular automata" in computer science, and they have been around for a while. Such systems are highly interconnected. Anything that happens to any dot changes what happens to all the others. Those changes then change the dot that started the process in the first place.

Interconnected systems like these have another name in mathematics and physics. They are called "complex dynamical systems": *complex* because of all those interconnections and *dynamical* because everything keeps changing all the time—each change causing more changes and so on. It's a kind of chaotic dance of changes.

Here is an "official" definition from the University of Alaska:

> Complex systems are characterized by non-trivial interaction between parts such that the entire system behaves different[ly] than just the sum of its parts. Examples include coupled neurons in the brain, ice-ocean-atmosphere coupling in the climate system, and interacting particles in solid, liquid or soft matter. Already the coupling of only two pendula yields collective behavior that cannot be understood from just the physics of one pendulum. Complex systems can be sensitive to small perturbations (chaotic) and reveal quite counterintuitive behavior ranging from stabilization by random events to unpredictable collapse of system behavior. (Wackerbauer, 2010)

Complex systems can show "emergent behavior" and "spontaneous order," like the flocking of birds or the formation of tornadoes. When complex systems move from chaos to order, we call them "self-organizing systems." You will hear a lot about these in the rest of this book.

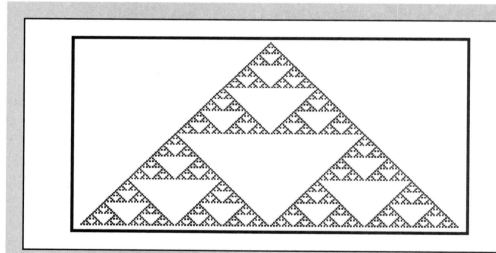

Figure 0.1 Sierpiński Triangles

Source: Mitra & Kumar (2006). Used with permission of Complex Systems Publications Inc.

Note: Starting with a single dot at the top central point of a blank rectangular space, Sierpiński triangles are produced, top downward, with a set of rules that govern what happens at each "time step" depending on the existence or not of each dot's neighbors on either side. Each step depends on the previous (past) step. There is nothing in the future for any step.

Now let's get back to our experiment.

Once we had the program working, we put just one dot at the bottom of the screen and let the program run. The screen filled with a beautiful pattern of triangles. But there was nothing in our program to make triangles!

In this system, each step was constructed from the dots of the previous step; the future was a blank that filled up as the past steps created the next steps.

But what if the future was not just a blank? What if the future had things in it already?

We presented our system with a situation in which the future "time steps" were already populated with an image—as though its future already existed. We put a smiley face in the future of our world of dots. Then we ran the program again. The dots "met" the future, and the screen became a chaos of dots, meaningless and pulsing with no pattern. And then. . . .

Suddenly, the chaos disappeared, and staring at us from the screen were not one but *three* smiley faces! The dots had made their imaginary future, happen.

If you want to learn more about our experiments, you can read our published work (see Mitra & Kumar, 2006).

Where did the smiley faces go, and how did they return? Maybe they didn't "go" anywhere; they were just spread through the system. Maybe they did not "return"; they were reborn! Maybe we're not asking the right questions.

In addition, all this is just a computer simulation; does it have any relationship to real life? I found that it does. Nature uses this sort of upside down causality quite often.

On a quiet surface of water, the water molecules are all connected to each other through molecular forces. You could disturb the quietness with a drop of water, dropped from a small height.

As the drop falls in, ripples form and move outward. And then, they move in. A bulge appears and the smooth surface of the water throws up a drop, exactly like the one that fell in. It is as though a memory is converted into an imagined future in which a drop, just like the first one, falls in again. Where did the water drop go, and how did it return?

Now you must not confuse this kind of "return" with a rather dubious theory called "water memory." I am not talking about water remembering things. I am talking about an input drop that gets distributed throughout the water and then reappears again in a show of spontaneous order.

If a future "exists," then it is actualized into the present and then into the past of the system. On the other hand, if an imagined future does not actually exist in the future but only in the present mind of the person imagining it, then we are not really talking about causality being symmetric in time. What we are talking about is "forward and backward causation." But there is only a fine, and somewhat semantic, difference between the two.

The reproduced water drop in the photo in Figure 0.3 (Frame 4) is clearly not the same as the one that was dropped in Frame 1. It cannot be. After all, the original drop would have merged with the water body, much as our smiley face picture in our simulation merged into the rest of the dots.

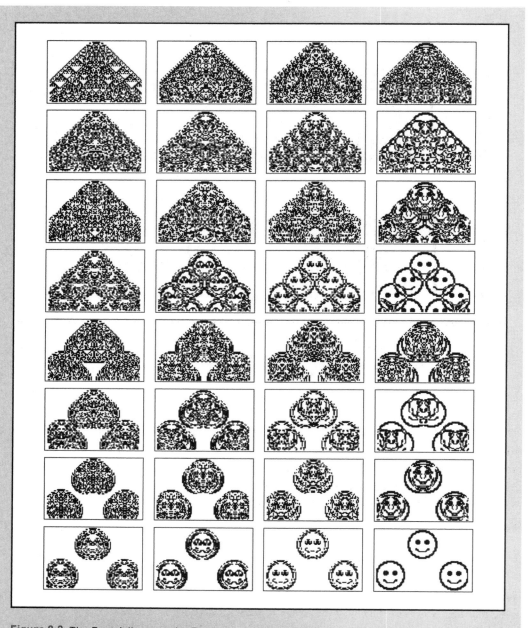

Figure 0.2 The Past Adjusts to the Future

Source: Mitra & Kumar (2006). Used with permission of Complex Systems Publications Inc.

Note: Starting with a single dot at the top center of a rectangular space, where a "smiley face" symbol is placed in the future, the same rules that were making the triangles earlier produced a chaotic pattern, which, as it evolved, reproduced the "smiley face" in multiple copies, over and over. Their future was actualized and became their past.

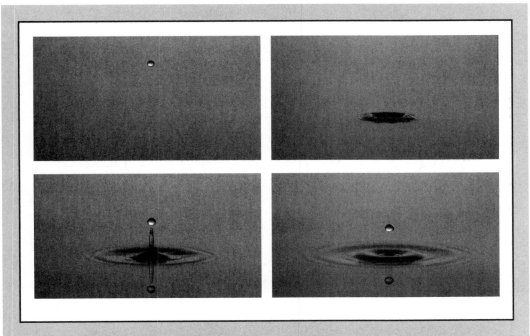

Figure 0.3 Water Memory?

Source: iStock.com/SoraPhotography

So the reproduced drop and the reproduced smiley faces were both creations from the mass of connected molecules in the water or dots in our simulation. They are "reincarnations" of the original intervention. I can't think of a better word to describe the "thing" that is produced by the system.

The reincarnated water drop would be identical (under perfect conditions) to the original drop that fell in.

So can water actually remember things? Now that seems completely absurd, and in any case, the word "remember" has too many human connotations

But if the mass of water was a connected system, like our cellular automata in the dots experiment, then it is easy to see how an input would be "remembered" and replicated. No magic there, just the nature of complex dynamical systems.

Suppose it was not a water drop that fell in but something else—something that is not water. Many people have filmed things falling into water in slow motion. I found one video from MIT that was from a particularly good camera. The video showed a tube-shaped metal object dropping into water.

The water body threw up a watery version of the intrusion, and, remarkably, what came out was rather like a copy of what fell in! Not quite, but weirdly so. This time, I could not call it a reincarnation; after all, it was made of something different from what fell in. I want to call it a "ghost."

Figure 0.4 Water Drop Replication in Water

Source: High Speed Imaging: Object dropping into water https://youtu.be/pLL6oseE5_U via YouTube

So can water molecules replicate what they "see" and "experience"? Was it the same mechanism at work that made our cellular automata experiment produce fractal images?

In gravitation, imagine a single object, alone in an empty universe. It does nothing. If it was moving to start with, it just keeps moving. If it was stationary to start with, it remains that way. Simple stuff.

Now add another object, and you have a "two-body" system. The two objects pull each other as they move, sometimes colliding, sometimes circling around each other. We can calculate exactly what will happen to them, over time. We can solve the two-body problem.

Now add a third object, and you get a three-body system. All three objects pull at each other simultaneously as they move. What results is a complex, dynamic, chaotic dance. We can no longer predict what will happen using mathematics. We can't solve the three-body problem. It is an old frustration of physicists and mathematicians. They call it the "many-body problem."

We just don't know what complex dynamical systems do, and how they do it.

SO ARE WE LIKE THAT?

Can the connected synapses of our brains sense and actualize a future? Indeed, can the immensely connected internet "see" and reproduce a future? Well, if our brains are complex dynamical systems, like those in the cellular automata experiment, then surely, they would show similar behavior. And the internet, another complex connected "system," might also realize a future. Let's think about this.

When you post or tweet, your message creates tiny changes in what others, connected to you, will post or tweet. Those changes will affect what your next post or tweet will be, and so on. The whole system will go chaotic until spontaneous order emerges. I am not guessing—anyone who has worked with complex systems will have experienced this. We just don't know how to calculate where the system will go or what the resulting order will look like—we don't have the math yet.

As a system, the brain or the internet comprises billions of objects, each affecting the other, almost simultaneously. Is the internet like a brain—a very big one? In the case of the brain, we sense that the whole network of neurons is more than the sum of its parts. We have a mind, and that seems to be more than the physical brain. Is there an internet "mind"? Just as it is not quite right to ask *where* the internet is, we don't ask *where* the mind is. Networks exist, but they are not anywhere. Are words such as "mind," "consciousness," or "learning" perhaps examples of spontaneous order, which we have not yet recognized? We don't know yet.

If we are part of a many-body system, if that system changes depending on its future as well as its past, then imagination is material in a strange, upside down kind of way. Our very existence then would depend on our ability to imagine a future.

In this book, you might glimpse a future of learning that is caused by such interconnectedness.

In this video excerpt from Jerry Rothwell's documentary *The School in the Cloud* (2018), you will hear Sugata Mitra speak about the complex dynamical systems we find in nature.

Video 0.1:
The Edge of Chaos

Videos may also be accessed at **resources .corwin.com/ schoolinthecloud**.

To read a QR code, you must have a smartphone or tablet with a camera. We recommend that you download a QR code reader app that is made specifically for your phone or tablet brand.

WHO WANTS TO KNOW ABOUT THE FUTURE OF LEARNING?

The thousands of teachers I know around the world are intensely interested in the future of learning because their jobs are changing and evolving. True, some are not interested because they think learning will continue to be the way it is. I hope they will read this book too.

Parents want to know what they should do about the future of learning. Many are confused today because they can see that their children are different, are in another time.

Educational leaders—people who head organizations that deal with teaching and learning—are looking for answers and perhaps will find some here. They should want to know what might happen to their institutions and organizations.

Researchers who are looking for answers to the big questions about learning will enjoy this book. What is learning? Why is it there? How does it work? What will happen to it?

Policy makers, politicians, and administrators—the people who make the future for this planet—need to know about the world in which learning may become unrecognizable from what it is today. In this new world, "knowing" itself may no longer mean what we think it does.

Engineers and architects need to know how to design schools for the future.

Technology developers need to know about the future of learning because their entire livelihoods depend on that future. What technologies will propel us into the future of learning? And what will pull us back into the past?

And we must not forget the learners themselves! For them, the future of learning determines their lives. They are the ones most affected by the future of learning, and, ironically, they will be the ones shaping that future.

All of us are learning all of the time. I hope the pages to follow will be useful for *everyone.*

THE SCHOOL IN THE CLOUD

A Chronology

1999	The Hole-in-the-Wall experiments begin
2000	
2001	
2002	
2003	The Hole-in-the-Wall experiments end
2004	
2005	*The Hole in the Wall* book is published
2006	The remoteness study is conducted
2007	Three SOLE projects begin: Kalikuppam, Hyderabad, and ATLAS
2008	
2009	The Granny Cloud and the Gateshead experiments begin
2010	The Gateshead experiments end
2011	The Hyderabad and ATLAS projects end
2012	*Beyond the Hole in the Wall*, an e-book, is published
2013	The School in the Cloud project begins
2014	
2015	
2016	
2017	The School in the Cloud project ends
2018	
2019	*The School in the Cloud* book is published

WHAT HAPPENS WHEN CHILDREN MEET THE INTERNET?

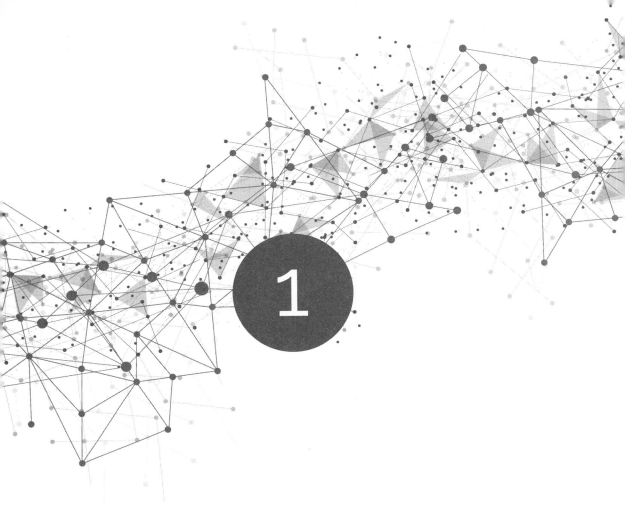

1

SELF-ORGANIZING
SYSTEMS IN LEARNING

Children, when given access to the internet in groups, can learn anything by themselves. Indeed, traditional "learning" itself may no longer be as important as it used to be. When I was in school, we "learned" how to find out what compounds a powder was made of. This used to be called "salt analysis" in my time. We had examinations during which we had to prove that we knew how to do this. We were given a small amount of a powder and asked to find out what it contained. We would spend hours dissolving bits of the powder in various acids and then adding other liquids, looking for precipitates, changes of color, and so on. Today, you would pop the powder into a machine, maybe a chromatograph or a spectrum analyzer, and it would tell you what is in the powder in minutes. Salt analysis was an amazing piece of Victorian chemistry. We learned to become chemical detectives. Since school, my brain has been trying to erase the knowledge of this now obsolete and unnecessary skill.

"

Children, when given access to the internet in groups, can learn anything by themselves.

In 1968, when Stanley Kubrick's film *2001: A Space Odyssey* came out, I was 16 years old. The film had a profound effect on me. What remains with me to this day is the notion that humankind, in the presence of something inexplicable, will focus all its energies and abilities on figuring out what that inexplicable thing is.

1999—THE HOLE IN THE WALL

The slums that sprawl behind the plush Balaji Estate of Kalkaji, a busy suburb of Delhi, contain the unauthorized shanties of the cleaners, house cleaners, auto rickshaw drivers, and servants who labor for the wealthy inhabitants of Kalkaji. These slums are home to thousands of children. There are a few government schools with listless, uninterested teachers. The children can barely read or write. They know almost no English. In those days before the third millennium, most had never seen a computer or heard of the internet.

It was here that I installed the first Hole in the Wall, a computer sunk into the opening of a wall with its screen facing the playground (a filthy patch of ground with an overflowing garbage dump where the children played). Within eight hours, children began to surf the web and to teach other children to surf the web. No adults were there to instruct them. They learned how to play games, paint, and how to look for information. They were able to learn some crude but workable English to enable them to do all this. You can read about the experiment in detail in my 2005 book, *The Hole in The Wall: Self Organising Systems in Education.*

Funded by the World Bank, ICICI Bank Limited, and the Government of Delhi, my research colleagues and I repeated the experiment many times over in the slums and villages of India. The results were always the same—digital literacy sprang out of seemingly nowhere.

The Ministry of External Affairs, Government of India, gifted five such "Hole-in-the-Wall" computer installations to Cambodia, and the Government of South Africa independently repeated the experiment in two places in South Africa. The results were the same. The measurement methods we used are described in detail in a 2005 paper (Mitra et al., 2005).

After the initial excitement settled down, we noticed that the children all began to use the internet for their homework. They copied down things from websites and took them to their astounded teachers. The children were, almost always, copying the right things down. How did they find the websites that were relevant? How did they find the right answers?

CAN CHILDREN LEARN
WITH TECHNOLOGY?

In another experiment, we later discovered that children's scores in English, math, and science became worse the further into remote and rural India we went (Mitra, Dangwal, & Thadani, 2008). Figure 1.1 shows the startling effect of distance on students' learning in these key subject areas. This finding makes sense when you consider that the best teachers are leaving rural areas to pursue better jobs and a higher quality of life closer to the city.

Ravi Bisht, traveling from village to village all across India, built several little structures with three computers facing the road. Sanjay Gupta, head of our Centre for Research in Cognitive Systems (CRCS), created a series of inventions that made sure the computers would continue to work in any environment. Bisht, Gupta, and their team invented new solid-state, touch-sensitive mice and protective covers for keyboards, and they reversed exhaust fans and added a thousand other vital little things that made it possible for ordinary PCs to work outdoors—anywhere. Another colleague, Himanshu, wrote software that would enable us to "see" our computers from anywhere using the internet and that prevented the Windows operating system from freezing or our hard drives from getting accidentally deleted. We did all this between 2000 and 2004.

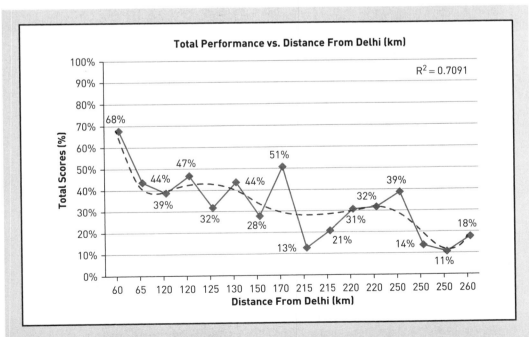

Figure 1.1 Test Scores as Related to Distance From Delhi

Source: Mitra, Dangwal, & Thadani (2008). *Australasian Journal of Educational Technology*, Vol. 24, No. 2.

In 22 locations and with 100 computers installed in remote villages, our field observers began their work. Focus groups were tested for nine months, and the results were compared with control groups and other frequent users. An estimated 40,000 children used these computers, and many of these children became computer literate all on their own. The computer literacy scores stood at an impressive 40 percent after just nine months (see Figure 1.2).

The published results of this study—proof that self-organized learning was possible—earned us the distinction of the American Educational Research Association (AERA) best paper of the year in 2005.

Years later, Ritu Dangwal reproduced the original Hole-in-the-Wall experiments in the mountain country of Bhutan. She took an overall sample size of 550 children (350 in the experimental group, 200 in the control group). Dangwal prudently renamed the Hole-in-the-Wall computers, calling them "learning stations." Despite the children in Bhutan having very different cultural attitudes toward technology and even less access to technology than the children in India, the rate of learning in both countries was nearly the same (see Figure 1.3; Mitra & Dangwal, 2017). In fact, the slopes of the Indian and the normalized Bhutanese

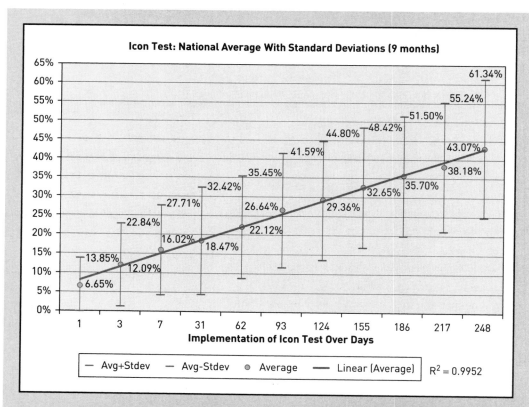

Figure 1.2 Growth in Computer Literacy Over a Nine-Month Period

Source: **Mitra et al. (2005).** *Australasian Journal of Educational Technology*, Vol. 21, No. 3.

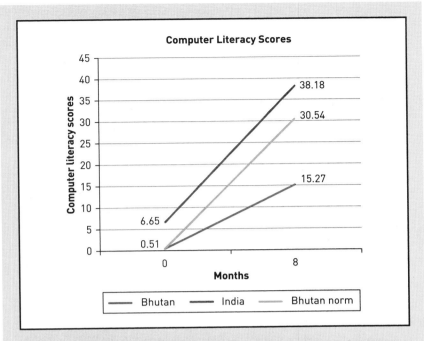

Figure 1.3 Computer Literacy Acquisition in Bhutan and India

Source: Mitra & Dangwal (2017). Springer Netherlands. CC BY 4.0.

scores are nearly identical in Figure 1.3. If the starting difference (Bhutan at 0.51, India at 6.65) were to be equalized, the two lines would overlap. These results are explained in more detail in Mitra and Dangwal (2017).

Could this be an indication that an identical learning mechanism was at work in both countries?

Our subsequent experiments over several years made it clear that groups of children, given access to the internet in safe and public spaces, will learn to use computers and the internet with no instructions from adults. Our experiments show that children in groups learn at greater rates than individual children working on their own. This collective hive mind proved to be an efficient teacher. It took me years to realize that this collective learning situation was an example of a self-organizing system—much like the water drop experiment—in which spontaneous order appears out of nowhere.

If you are a parent or guardian of children, let them access the internet on a big screen in groups in a shared public space (such as a living room). Give the internet the same status you give your TV set. Get ready to see miraculous learning happening!

Our subsequent experiments over several years made it clear that groups of children, given access to the internet in safe and public spaces, will learn to use computers and the internet with no instructions from adults.

Twenty years later, I realized that the computer in the wall was like the monolith at the dawn of humankind in the opening scenes of Clarke's *2001: A Space Odyssey*. It was a pointer, a compass, a weathervane. I can see now that it was pointing at a rather strange future.

2007—THE GATESHEAD EXPERIMENTS

Newcastle upon Tyne is a small and pretty town, south of Scotland. On one side of the River Tyne is Newcastle; on the other is Gateshead. The people here are often called Geordies. They have a distinct dialect that is quite hard to understand. Newcastle was the hub of British industry in the eighteenth and nineteenth centuries. It is here that the ships to take settlers to the New World of America were built. It is here that the coal to fire the boilers on those ships was mined.

One day, from here, education would change, the world over.

In November 2006, I was appointed Professor of Educational Technology at Newcastle University. At the age of 54, I moved to England after a lifetime in India. I had no idea what a professor did, so I smiled vacuously at whomever I met or passed. I thought I would spend a few pleasant years in England and then retire. But then, in January 2009, the film *Slumdog Millionaire* upset everything. *Slumdog Millionaire* is based on the novel *Q & A* by Vikas Swarup. The film won many Oscars and a Golden Globe award and was in the news for quite a while, when an Indian newspaper asked Swarup what had inspired him to write the book.

Swarup was candid: "I was inspired by the hole-in-the-wall project, where a computer with an internet connection was put in a Delhi slum. When the slum was revisited after a month, the children of that slum had learnt how to use the worldwide web. That got me fascinated and I realised that there's an innate ability in everyone to do something extraordinary, provided they are given an opportunity. How else do you explain children with no education at all being able to learn to use the internet? This shows knowledge is not just the preserve of the elite," Swarup said, while talking about the project, in which NIIT chief scientist Dr. Sugata Mitra had carved a hole in the wall that separated the NIIT premises from the adjoining slum in Kalkaji in 1999. Through this hole, a freely accessible computer was put out for use and with no prior experience, the children learnt to use the computer on their own. (Roy, 2009)

I had inspired the book that became the film! NIIT University in India and Newcastle University, UK, went berserk, as though *they* had won the Golden Globes. I had newspaper reporters and TV crews crawling all over my office.

What happened next would affect the whole world and propel my research even further. It started with an email on May 14, 2009.

Hi, Professor Mitra,

I hope you don't mind me getting in touch with you like this, but I wanted to see if it was possible to find out more about your research involving children and ICT.

I recently saw a DVD of a talk that you gave at British Airways, where my husband works, and was fascinated by your story.

I am a Primary School teacher (Year 4, Age 8–9), working in an area of social deprivation (St. Aidan's Primary, Teams, Gateshead). We are about to receive laptops for our children to use in our classrooms, and would love it if you could come into our school to share your research findings on minimally invasive education with us.

I have spoken with my Head Teacher, Mrs. Lesley Steele, who was keen that I contact you to find out if this would be possible. We are a forward thinking school and are always keen to take on new ideas that put children at the centre of their own learning.

I feel that our children, and staff, would benefit greatly from your approach to children's learning.

Thanks,
Emma Crawley

Emma's email sparked my curiosity: Would the findings from the poorest children in the world have any meaning in this, one of the richest and most developed countries in the world?

Barrie Craven, my friend and colleague at Newcastle, and I had found children in poorer areas performing worse than those in affluent areas (Mitra, 2009).

Remoteness was a problem in England too. Only it was another kind of remoteness. Socioeconomic remoteness, cultural remoteness, ethnic remoteness—all existed inside the affluent cities of England. Craven took subsidized housing in England as an indicator of economic disadvantage and found that General Certificate of Secondary Education (GCSE) exam results would be poorer where more poor people lived, as illustrated in Figure 1.4.

I spoke to the teachers at St. Aidan's Church of England Primary School about the Hole in the Wall and associated experiments. They were excited, and the head teacher and principal, Mrs. Lesley Steele, invited me back to meet the children.

St. Aidan's is a small school in Gateshead, England. I met the children of Year 4 (about eight years old) in July 2009. It was an immense relief. Suddenly, the differences between continents and peoples disappeared. We became good friends, Year 4 and I. Eight-year-olds are the same everywhere, no matter what the circumstances.

> *Eight-year-olds are the same everywhere, no matter what the circumstances.*

"Do you want to ask Sugata anything about India?" asked Emma. The children nodded vigorously.

"Do they have chips in India?" asked a boy.

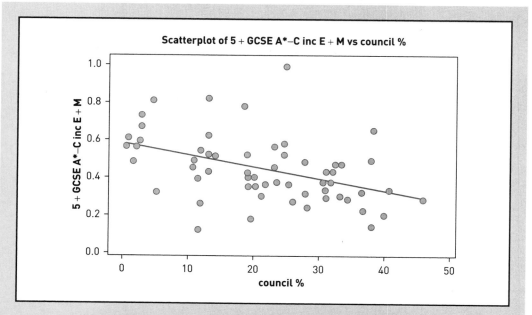

Figure 1.4 The Effect of Subsidized Housing Density on Exam Performance

Source: Mitra (2009).

"Of course, they have chips! Can't you think of anything other than chips?" asked an exasperated Emma.

That afternoon, when it was time for the school day to end, the children queued to leave their classroom. "Want to try something?" I asked.

"YES," they chorused.

I asked every alternate child to face the other way from the one in front. So the first child faced the door, the second turned to face away from the door, and so on.

"So, do we have one line or two?" I asked.

"One line, all topsy-turvy"; "No, two lines"; "It's not a line at all" . . . there was bedlam. Then came a clear and loud voice from a little girl.

"There are two opposite lines in the same place, together," she said. I looked at Emma, and she made a face, muttering, "Quantum physics or what!" The bell rang, and the two-lines-that-were-one marched away to the waiting parents.

I emailed Emma again with another idea.

Hi Emma:

This is what I thought we could try:

1. *Take a GCSE exam question on the environment*

2. *Ask the children to work on it in groups of 4 using the internet, but no help from us.*

3. *See what happens.*

4. *Repeat the question in 2 months, without the internet, and see how much is retained.*

The question could be as below:

Give the main survival advantage of each of the following adaptations:

For example, a rabbit's large ears allow it to hear predators from far away.

a. *A polar bear's white coat;*

b. *A hedgehog's spikes;*

c. *A cheetah's bendy spine;*

d. *An eagle's sharp claws;*

e. *A lion's powerful teeth.*

(Marks available: 5)

Answer outline and marking scheme for question: 1

a. *Camouflaged body so its prey doesn't see it creeping up in the snow;*

b. *Protection from predators;*

c. *Flexibility allows the cheetah to reach its maximum speed quickly and smoothly;*

d. *So it can dive down and grab its prey quickly and not drop it;*

e. *So it can tear and grind meat easily.*

Would you like to try this? [. . .]

Regards,
Sugata

On July 6, 2009, with great enthusiasm, the 24 children of Year 4 attempted five GCSE questions, four years ahead of their time. These were questions about the survival advantage of adaptation, as I had suggested. We asked the children to use a few computers, about one for every four children, and told them they could do whatever they liked, talk to whomever they liked, and move around if they wanted to. I explained to Emma that I was trying to replicate the environment of the Hole-in-the-Wall computers in India. We, Emma and I, vanished into the background in a corner of the classroom. In about 30 minutes, groups of children started to come up with their answers on pieces of paper. After all the groups had submitted, I asked each group to make up a question they liked and have everyone else answer that question individually, without the internet. Then I left, instructing Emma to retain the answers and repeat the questions after two months, with the children answering individually without use of the internet. Then I told her to mark all the answers, tabulate the results, and contact me—it's just the way we professors do things, you see.

On July 9, Emma wrote to me with the results of the first test:

Here are the results:

GCSE question

> *Group 1: 5 points*
>
> *Group 2: 5 points*
>
> *Group 3: 4 points*
>
> *Group 4: 3 points (only answered 3 questions)*
>
> *Group 5: 2 points (only answered 3 questions; one of answers given—polar bears don't have white fur!! This was the group that children were reluctant to work in!)*

Self-organised test

> *7 children 1/5*
>
> *13 children 2/5*
>
> *2 children 3/5*
>
> *1 child 4/5*
>
> *1 child 5/5*

[She meant that in the test constructed by children, out of five questions, 7 children got one right, 13 got two right, and so on.]

Hope this is of interest to you.

What could we observe from this data? That groups can answer GCSE questions, years ahead of time. And, after learning in groups, many individuals can assimilate the answers into personal understanding. But would they retain what they had encountered?

Emma followed our experimental plan and retested the children individually. She wrote on October 7, 2009, more than two months after the initial experiment:

Hi Sugata,

. . . . I tested the children last week and here are the results.

> *23 children tested*
>
> *5/5: 9 children*
>
> *4/5: 7 children*
>
> *3/5: 5 children*
>
> *2/5: 2 children*

Quite impressive I think. The answers were well written with accurate vocab. I tried to mark as I had in the original group task. The children completed the test very quickly and with no problems.

Hope this is useful to you.

I checked carefully and confirmed that the children had not been "taught" anything at all about this subject in the intervening months. How did they do even better, months later, than they had on the first day? I was a bit taken aback. To me this was "anomalous learning"—not something you would expect. The results of this small study provided another weathervane pointing at the future of learning.

A little secret: When water is cooled, it contracts in volume as expected. But below 4 degrees centigrade, it starts to expand again. This is called "anomalous expansion." End of secret.

Over the course of the next academic year, we conducted a series of experiments. The Year 4 students became supremely confident, so we decided to make the questions harder. They did GCSE A-Level questions (normally given in Year 12!), laughing and shouting all the time. Figure 1.6 shows a glimpse of the data.

When this study was published in 2014, I posted the online link to it on my Twitter feed. At the time, I had 20,000 followers, many of them teachers. Several teachers read the paper and started replicating the results in their own classrooms. They said it worked exactly as I had described it—most of the time. This was my first experience of the power of social media in science. Teachers don't usually read academic journals; they usually don't have the time or inclination. But platforms such as Twitter and Facebook give teachers the chance to take a quick glance at research studies to find out if the findings relate to their own work.

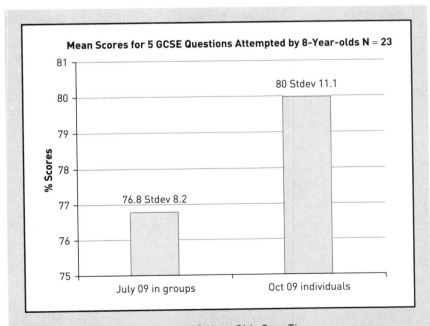

Figure 1.5 Learning Retention of 8-Year-Olds Over Time

Source: Mitra & Crawley (2014).

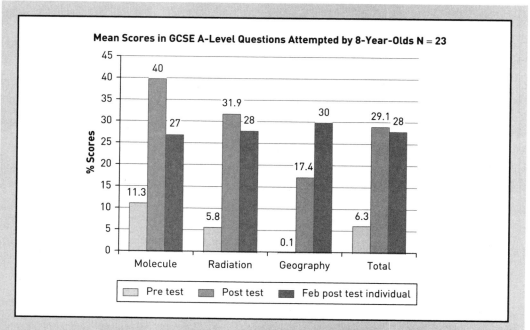

Figure 1.6 8-Year-Olds Doing the Work of 17-Year-Olds and Retaining Information Over Time

Source: Mitra & Crawley (2014).

I had to invent a name for this learning "method"—I could not call it the "Hole in the Wall" anymore because it was not in any wall. It was now inside classrooms. But in these classrooms order was replaced by mild chaos in the hope of an emergent spontaneous order. I found another name for what we had done. We had discovered the "Self-Organized Learning Environment" (SOLE).

During 2008 to 2009, while working with Emma Crawley's students, I was traveling back and forth between Gateshead, England, and India. In India, my colleagues and I were setting up the first SOLEs (self-organized learning environments) as computer labs in Indian schools. We had no funding except for my lecture fees from keynote speeches at conferences.

2009—THE GRANNY CLOUD

Our many experiments over the course of several years indicated that groups of children (all types of children, in a variety places, speaking a diverse set of languages), given free and public access to computers and the internet, can

1. become computer literate on their own—learn to use computers and the internet for most of the tasks done by lay users;

2. teach themselves enough English to use email, chat, and search engines;

3. learn to search the internet for answers to questions in a few months' time;

4. improve their English pronunciation on their own;

5. improve their mathematics and science scores in school; and

6. evaluate opinions and detect indoctrination and propaganda.

Our new driving question became "Is there a limit to what children can understand using the internet?"

ADMIRATION AS PEDAGOGY: THE KALIKUPPAM EXPERIMENT

In an effort to answer this new question, Ritu Dangwal and I conducted our next experiment in Kalikuppam, a village in southern India, in 2010. We designed a question that we thought the children couldn't possibly answer: What is the process of DNA replication? So can 12-year-old Tamil-speaking children in Kalikuppam learn and understand DNA replication, in English, from a Hole-in-the-Wall computer, without guidance from an adult?

To my amazement, the answer was yes!

In a Hole-in-the-Wall computer, we downloaded university-level material on biotechnology. We tested random samples of children after two months and compared the results with a private school in Delhi where the same material was taught by a trained biotechnology teacher.

In Kalikuppam, the children had progressed from a near zero score to about 30 percent, just by themselves. This in itself is astounding considering that they were researching in a language they barely understood, with a topic that was years ahead of what was traditionally taught at their age. But I wanted to know if I could get them to a higher score. What would that take? Should I get a teacher?

Since there was no way to find a biochemistry teacher in Kalikuppam, I decided to use a "mediator." This person was just a friendly adult figure who would encourage them to go further through simple heartening statements such as "My goodness, how did you understand that?" or "I could never understand that by myself!" and that sort of thing—very similar to how a grandmother might admire her grandchildren. The mediator had no subject knowledge. She had affection for the children, and she admired them. I called this the "method of the grandmother." In a few weeks, the method of the grandmother got the children of Kalikuppam to the same level as older children who were taught by a trained biochemistry teacher in an urban school in Delhi (see Figure 1.7).

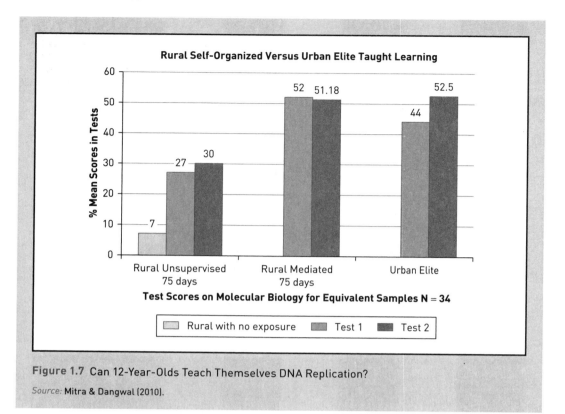

Figure 1.7 Can 12-Year-Olds Teach Themselves DNA Replication?

Source: Mitra & Dangwal (2010).

Kalikuppam taught us two very important lessons.

1. **We need to share this message.** Just before joining Newcastle University, in 2006, I had spoken at the Pan Commonwealth Forum (PCF) in Jamaica. My description of self-organized learning was politely called "naïve." After the Kalikuppam experiment (2010), I started using a new slide in my lectures. It said, "Children given access to the internet in groups, can learn anything by themselves." That statement was no longer called naïve; it was called dangerous. As long as you are naïve, you can be ignored; when you are dangerous, you start to be attacked.

2. **Admiration is a powerful learning tool.** Self-organized learning is helped along by admiration! I called this method "minimally invasive education."

I thought the granny method showed promise, and I wanted to try it again. Could it be just as effective over Skype? Would this technology allow parents and children in remote villages access to the kind of education they desired?

Watch Video 1.1: Krishanu. In this video excerpt from Rothwell's *The School in the Cloud* (2018), you can hear Krishanu's parents talk about the kind of education that is available to their son and the kind of education they want for him.

Video 1.1:
Krishanu

Videos may also
be accessed at
**resources
.corwin.com/
schoolinthecloud.**

SKYPE GRANNIES

After *Slumdog Millionaire*, Lucy Tobin (2009) from *The Guardian* interviewed me, titling her piece "Slumdog Professor," a name that has stuck.

Toward the end of the article, she wrote the following:

> He has also set up computers installed with telephony-service Skype in schools in Hyderabad, and has a similar set-up near his office in Newcastle for a particularly innovative initiative. "When I last visited India, I asked the children what they would like to use Skype for most, and surprisingly they said they wanted British grandmothers to read them fairy tales—they'd even worked out that between them they could afford to pay £1 a week out of their own money," says Mitra.

The editor of *The Guardian* put in the following line at the end of the article:

> Anyone wanting to participate in fairytale reading sessions needs a broadband connection, a clear voice, and a few hours a week. Contact: sugata.mitra@newcastle.ac.uk

Within days of publication, emails started pouring in.

My colleague Mabel Quiroga from Buenos Aires put together a list of the volunteers. To offer our new volunteers some guidance, I put together a brief, called the "method of the grandmother":

- Do not teach.

- Have a conversation.

- Raise questions and ask the children to work out possible answers.

In other words, they can conduct a SOLE (self-organized learning environment) session over Skype. As Granny Jackie Barrow later put it, "A session is not a lesson."

We decided to call this group of volunteers "The Granny Cloud." The members chose to call themselves "Cloud Grannies" irrespective of their gender or age.

Mabel put together a hurried webpage for the Granny Cloud to use and schedule sessions. To keep the operations going, I requested Suneeta Kulkarni from Pune, India, to monitor the scheduling and usage. She went on to become "Director of the Granny Cloud."

Video 1.2:
Gateshead Granny
Cloud

Videos may also
be accessed at
**resources
.corwin.com/
schoolinthecloud**.

The development of the Granny Cloud proceeded in fits and starts.

The first applicants were Judith Sismey, Hazel Dakers, Val Almond, Liz Fewings, Anne Thomas, Rosemary Noble, Diane Nadalini, Helen Schofield, Jackie Barrow. To me, these are important names in the history of children's education.

Jackie Barrow in particular has become one of the most influential Grannies in our community. Jackie lives near Manchester, UK. She can clearly pronounce "Llanfairpwllgwyngyllgogerychwyrndrobwllllantysiliogogogoch" (the name of a village in Wales). Can anyone ask for more?

Since that time, Jackie has interacted with thousands of children in India and elsewhere. I am very fortunate to know her.

Between 2009 and 2011, the Granny Cloud matured and evolved. It also gained worldwide visibility with the Cloud Grannies blogging about their sessions.

You can find many references to the Granny Cloud on YouTube and Facebook by searching "Granny Cloud." You can also find examples and materials on the Granny Cloud website (www.thegrannycloud.org) and the Granny Cloud Facebook Group. One particularly good example is a seven-minute video called *Gateshead Granny Cloud*.

One of the Grannies, Sue Duckworth, offered this brief description of a Granny session:

> Ten eager faces awaited me at MANAS red group two weeks ago. We recapped on what we did last week. They all remembered and it was discussing bees. I had emailed them a poem, "The Honeybee," to carry on the theme. They individually read this to me, which took up quite a lot of the time allotted. I then showed them how to make origami birds. We soon had birds flying in the classroom. They really seem to enjoy this. All too soon our time was over, and the children waved me a cheery goodbye (Granny Cloud Facebook Group, 2018).

In 2010, the Cloud Grannies started to have (physical) conferences—including one in London and a big one in India in 2016—during which they visited some of the sites where they had Skyped. Children of the remote sites in India that they went too were amazed to find their Cloud Grannies were real after all. The Granny Cloud is now active all over the world, from India to Greenland and from Britain to Colombia. The immense influence of these "clouds" on children is only just beginning to be documented.

In 2016, when I suggested raising some funds for a new Granny website, the core team declined the offer. Then members of that team said they could handle things themselves. It was a moment of joy for me, like the day a child leaves home. Toward the end of 2016, without any input or involvement from me, thegrannycloud.org came online. I never got a login invitation. The Granny Cloud had come of age.

"

"First they ignore you.
Then they ridicule you. And
then they attack you and want
to burn you. And then they build
monuments to you."

THE HYDERABAD PROJECT, 2007–2009

Our three-year research project in Hyderabad, India, investigated possible technological and pedagogical interventions to improve the quality of private schooling for the poor. It was funded by Prof. James Tooley of Newcastle University. I was traveling back and forth between England and India, as the Gateshead experiments were also in progress then.

Hyderabad is a bustling metropolis of 8 million people. In the 1990s, Hyderabad became a hub for software and information technology industries. It provides software engineers to much of the world. The older parts of the city consist of sprawling slums, where small shop owners, auto rickshaw drivers, and casual laborers live.

We based our work on the premise that there are places where good schools do not exist and good teachers cannot or do not wish to go. Under such circumstances, can children help themselves learn, without a school or teachers?

A Note on Privacy:

Parents should keep this in mind. A computer at home with a large screen placed in a public area, such as the one where the family watches TV, will generally be used in socially acceptable ways. I think it may help to get children used to this kind of internet access rather than peering at tiny, private screens when they are alone. The same probably holds true for grown-ups!

We found that if children work on large, publicly visible screens, there is not much need for any filter or other policing mechanisms to prevent "misuse" (usually a euphemism for access to internet pornography or other undesirable images). Groups of heterogeneous children, that is, boys and girls together, working in a public space where any passersby can see what they are doing, tend to focus on things that will not get them into trouble.

Our SOLEs were designed with nine computers with broadband and internet access. This accommodated up to 36 children.

The computers were often in clusters of three, creating a circular arrangement, which further facilitates interaction in a larger group (see Figure 1.8). Children could work in groups, access the internet and other software, follow up on a class activity or project, or go where their interests led them. It created opportunities for learners to search for curriculum-related or other information.

We put in all manner of "useful" software that we thought would help the children learn English, math, and other school subjects. Suneeta noticed in a few weeks that whenever children were given free access, spontaneous searches, rather than planned activities, were common. Throughout the Hyderabad project, we discovered interesting changes and progress in four particular areas: children's use of the internet, aspirations, English language development, and self-organizing behavior.

Use of the Internet

The children's teachers did not often allow them free access to the internet for fear that they would only "play games." In a bid to see what would happen if children

Figure 1.8 A SOLE Lab in Hyderabad

Can you spot the errors in design?

were challenged to search for answers to specific questions, four of the SOLEs tried an exercise involving a GCSE-level question. One of the striking findings in that exercise was that the Grade 3 children had never had access to the internet and hence were unaware of the concept of "searching" it.

So, in November 2009, in another SOLE with slightly older children (from Grades 5 to 7) a "search" activity was tried out to see if it had potential. These children too had minimal previous exposure to the internet. Games had been accessed from links to sites left on the computer by other groups of older children. However, this was the first time they had used Google search or other search engines. Challenged to find the "tallest building in the world," children enthusiastically began to figure out how to use a search engine to get information. This was the starting point. Scans of children's answers indicate their ability to use search engines after a very short exposure, though their limited fluency in English severely affected their understanding of what they accessed.

The exercise was taken further by encouraging them to search for the answers to questions in their own textbook, preferably from a lesson they were currently doing in class. Again, it was a task they undertook with eager participation and scans indicated they were able to locate the "right" answer.

The key is to pique children's curiosity continuously. Children will rise to the challenge.

SPONTANEOUS SEARCH

November 28, 2008

Some groups of children are beginning to use Google search to find things. A group of boys Grade 7–8 [Hidayath, Azeem, Yaseem. . . .] were observed looking at a picture of the human body. When asked what they were searching for, they said "bones" and although there was a link to anatomy, they did not appear to know that might be a relevant one. By chance, they clicked on the word "red" and went into a completely different site, seemed to realize that it was not what they were looking for [it showed the color red, flowers, etc.] and came back to the original site. . . . They later found some pictures of brain, kidney, ears. Another group of boys sitting at the adjacent terminal were looking on interestedly and when I approached them, said they also knew how to search. This capacity of the children was unknown to the school principal. When the information was shared with her, she smacked her head in a combination of wonder and surprise, with happiness.

Aspirations

One of the most striking changes that began to show up early in the project period had to do with the kinds of interests and aspirations the children expressed for themselves and what they hoped to see in their future. Stories like the ones from Suneeta's observations illustrate the powerful impact SOLEs had on children's aspirations.

English Language Development

Once we introduced mediators (Grannies) from other countries, we noticed significant gains in English language comprehension. The Grannies were native speakers of English from far off locales such as France, Sri Lanka, and Australia. Using Skype video, they read stories to the children and communicated with them in easy conversations full of expression so that the students could learn the natural pronunciation and cadence of the language. Suneeta saw children as young as five and six, during the course of their very first Skype interaction, "imitating" and enthusiastically mouthing words they found interesting over and over again!

Self-Organizing Behavior

An observation of particular interest given the premise of "*self-organizing*" is to see the principle in action.

Suneeta recorded several aspects of the effects of SOLEs on the social skills of children. She recorded the types of interactions among the children, the conflicts that invariably arose, and the methods the children evolved to resolve these conflicts. Sharing, taking turns, and subtle exercise of authority were all evident in the children's interactions. In particular, the children's ability to interact with people at a distance was noticeable.

MAKING THEIR OWN RULES

May 17, 2009

Suneeta reports:

Just a day after the opening of the SHS SOLE ([at] Shirgaon High School, in the state of Maharash-tra in western India), approximately 10 children were observed already in the SOLE in the early morning. Several more joined them as the day wore on and continued with their exploration of Paint, Google Earth, and Google Maps, etc.

One of the boys, Rajat, downloaded games with a pen drive he had gotten from a cousin living in the city. Unfortunately, it also downloaded a virus, which stalled the functioning of the internet. Understandably, most of the children were quite upset, but the children resolved the difficulty by creating the rule that "no pen drives were to be allowed."

Source: Kulkarni & Mitra (2010).

At the end of the project timeline in 2010, Suneeta observed that the schools still had no clarity about the purpose of SOLEs. Neither did the parents. The facilities were often closed and were poorly maintained. Hygienic conditions were appalling. The furniture was used at will in other parts of the school. As a result of these factors, the SOLEs simply weren't available to children as often as they should have been. The most frustrating part of the experiment was that we weren't able to give the students as much access to the SOLEs as we would have liked because we didn't have support from the schools where the SOLEs were located.

Suneeta and I decided to repeat the experiments that had been conducted in England in Hyderabad as faithfully as we could. We attempted to replicate the same GCSE questions that had been tried in Gateshead with samples of children from the Hyderabad schools. We were not successful in reproducing a single result! However, in the end, we did learn a lot from the Hyderabad project about things that we should not do. But the Hyderabad project was over and we needed a new project to continue to test our conclusions.

Serendipitously, Sumantra Roy, a successful young entrepreneur from Calcutta, contacted me.

THE ATLAS LEARNING CENTRE (ALC) IN GOSAVI VASTI, INDIA, 2012

Suneeta and I shared our conclusions from the Hyderabad experiences with Sumantra Roy. For a SOLE to work, we needed to provide children with

- reading comprehension skills in English, or a language with a large presence on the internet;

- adequate and free access to computers and the internet; and

- access to an organization willing to use this approach.

The experience with the SOLEs in Hyderabad underlined the importance of access and indicated that this was often difficult to achieve in the context of schools that operated in a typical authoritarian manner and possibly felt intimidated by this student-run (self-organized) approach.

Wanting to help children learn, Sumantra was eager to fund an experiment to study the development of reading skills in stand-alone SOLEs that were not associated with schools.

We set up the first stand-alone SOLE in 2010 at Talere, in western India, a rural area with relatively good internet connectivity. Initial assessments indicated that English reading and comprehension skills were almost completely absent. Children recognized the alphabet and the occasional word; some of the older children appeared to be able to read simple stories. However, they could not explain what they had read even in their native language.

The local community was very welcoming of our efforts. A core group of 20 children used the facility for several months. We drew some important lessons from this pilot:

- We can offer children free and adequate access to SOLEs via independent organizations.

- Although games are popular with children, there is no need for them to learn how to read or understand English to be successful at most games because they quickly learn how to achieve success through trial and error, even if the instructions are in English.

- In order to be motivated to read and understand English, the content offered needed to impact the children's lives at home or in school.

- Access alone is not enough to bring about a change in reading skills. Here was a challenge!

The Gosavi Vasti Atlas Learning Centre SOLE is located in a room in an urban slum. It is a rough area, where you will frequently hear squabbles and verbal abuse as you walk around. You will see residents playing cards and drinking just outside the "houses" that are made up of rough flooring and tin roofs.

The SOLE is housed in a small, 10 × 12 foot room that can accommodate two computers. The room has two small windows, tin roofing, and a rough and uneven floor. The children who come to the Gosavi Vasti ALC SOLE live in the neighboring urban slum. They range in age from 8 to 14 and typically attend the SOLE as a heterogeneous, mixed-age group.

The children are typically aggressive and quick to hit each other for even mild conflicts. Although the children are street smart and savvy, they do not have readiness for learning skills. The opportunity for the children to play on the computer is attractive to parents and children alike, given the very limited resources at home, and at school.

Earliest observations indicated that some of the children could not even recognize the English alphabet easily, but, typically, they were able to identify a few words such as "cat," "dog," and "ball" with effort. They could not recognize many more English words. Hence, the children could be classified as practically illiterate in English.

Suneeta decided on a course of minimal intervention to encourage children to engage with English. In a 90-minute session, the children could play games for an hour if they would spend the first 30 minutes exploring something new. Would they have done so anyway, without the imposed requirement, as the children in the Hole-in-the-Wall experiments did, given enough time? We will never know—we did not have that kind of time.

The minimal structure involved encouraging children to explore anything they wished from a number of recommended sites during the first 30 minutes using online resources and previously downloaded material, including games; listening to stories or songs; and playing games of their own choice from "half a dozen" selected or recommended sites.

The placement of the "semistructured" time was a critical aspect of the intervention since initial observations in May 2012 showed that placing it at the end of the session did not work. Typically, children would not stop playing the two or three games with which they had become familiar to try anything else out.

After several months, the children began to read.

Talere closed down sometime in 2011, and Gosavi's location struggled with gathering resources but have kept themselves alive on a month-to-month basis. Since 2017, they began interacting with the Grannies regularly. The local communities are trying, as far as I know, to collect funds to revive and maintain them. The dominant perspective there is still "Education without teachers? Rubbish!"

The biggest impediments to self-organized learning are that mediocre schools and poor parents cannot make or accept the conceptual jump to see the value in SOLEs and what children can learn while working in them. We failed to convey an understanding of the mission that would allow school leaders and parents to let go of their adherence to tradition that didn't allow anything new. I knew SOLEs had a chance of succeeding in mediocre schools and in poor areas as long as the community shared a common vision and faith in the ability of children to learn on their own.

A social scientist from the Netherlands, Payal Arora, on a visit to India in 2009 found a derelict site of one of my 2002 Hole-in-the-Wall experiments. She wrote a tear-jerking paper about how the empty hole in the wall (the computer had been removed after funding ran out) stared at her like an empty eye socket (see Arora, 2010). Donald Clark, a blogger, then wrote a scathing piece about how the "hole-in-the-wall . . . rarely worked" (Clark 2013).

They say, when you hit the bottom, there is only one way to go—upward. SOLEs surfaced and burst into the world again, like a huge, turbulent bubble—from Down Under.

"

"I would rather have
questions that can't be
answered than answers that
can't be questioned."

Attributed to Richard Feynman

2010—WHEN THE RUBBER HITS THE ROAD: IMPLEMENTATION AROUND THE WORLD

In yet another example of spontaneous order, a single event in Australia prompted SOLEs to begin spreading around the world.

Melbourne, Australia

I received an email, in 2010, from the Deputy Secretary, Office for Government School Education, Victoria, Australia, requesting I speak in front of the 3,500 principals and assistant principals who lead 1,600 of Victoria's government schools. It was the first time a government had contacted me. It was a turning point for SOLEs in the world.

The event, called the Big Day Out (2010), took place in Melbourne. It was the largest audience I had ever spoken to at that time. On this trip, I got the opportunity to visit several schools in and around Melbourne and, after my talk, to conduct SOLE demonstrations in them. As they have always done for me, the children stole the show.

I asked the children questions: "What's lightning? What makes the sky produce such a massive light and sound show?"

The 10-year-olds took just 15 minutes to come up with their first answers—separation of charges, ionization, and discharge. But had they understood anything? I could see the gleam of triumph in some of the watching teachers' eyes. "See, they are just parroting Google," I could hear them think.

I asked a girl what separation of charges meant. She didn't know, and I told her it was OK to ask her friends.

A whispered conversation ensued. "Positive and negative charges attract each other, so if you keep them apart, they want to meet as soon as they can," she declared.

"The air gets ionized into negative and positive charges called ions," said a boy from the back. "And they come back together really fast—BOOM!" Everybody laughed.

"My goodness! So that's what causes lightning?" I said. "But what are these ions you spoke about?" Nobody knew.

"OK, we can't get this close and give up, can we? Why don't you figure out what ions are?"

A bedlam of website visits, conversations, and group reorganization ensued. There were four computers and 20 children. The watching teachers were muttering among themselves. One of them came up to me and said, "There is an Aborigine girl in the class; should we provide any special attention for her?"

"No, let's just leave them alone," I said, mentally keeping all my fingers and toes crossed.

Thirty minutes passed and the children said they were ready to tell us. Four of them came up to the front of the room. A girl described how electrons can get stripped off or added to atoms to create ions.

"The net charge on an ion equals the total number of protons minus the total number of electrons in the atom concerned," she ended with a grin.

A pair of little hands held up a drawing with colored swirls and circles, showing protons and electrons with the bulge of an extra electron swelling out.

It was the Aborigine girl.

"When she understands something, she always draws it," said the talkative boy from the back. The children had a better understanding of her culture than the teachers and I did.

Later, back in England, I heard from Brett Millott, principal of Glenroy West Primary School, and Paul Kenna, principal of Belle Vue Park Primary School, who had been at the Big Day Out in Melbourne.

[. . .] A principal colleague and I have used Hole in the Wall teaching in two of our Year 5 classes at school, and the results were absolutely breath-taking.

The students researched the Black Plague, its causes and effects, and the way in which it changed society. The students found out an enormous amount of content in a very short time. They also learnt how to collaborate effectively.

The only thing we did was to pose the question and hand out markers so that the kids could share useful websites on our whiteboard.

At the end of the session, the students didn't want to stop working, and lots of them continued their studies at home. They also said that they felt smart, clever, and strong, and enjoyed the difficulty and freedom of the task.

Thanks for your inspiration,
Brett Millott
Principal
Glenroy West Primary School

It felt very good to hear this. I sent copies of Brett's letter to teachers in India and the UK. Emma, Suneeta, and Ritu responded as though they had just seen a football goal scored.

Brett and Paul continued with SOLEs, and I joined in on my visits to Melbourne. In a few months, the children of Victoria showed us the way.

We thought it might be useful to update you on our progress with Hole in the Wall Learning. Some of our Grade 5/6 teachers are now beginning to trial HITWL as one of the strategies of instruction in their classrooms.

We have begun to spread our trial across the senior classes at both of our schools, and the increase in student engagement and enthusiasm has been evident in every session.

Paul and I have been discussing how HITWL fits in so well with the Northern Metropolitan Regional Powerful Learning Project.

Over the next twelve to eighteen months, the third component of the Powerful Learning strategy (curiosity) will be introduced to bring further improvement to student learning.

For us the concepts of curiosity and student engagement run a parallel course, and your strategies have really struck a chord with us.

The direction set by Northern Region aligns closely with our interests in this topic, and we are keen to continue our relationship with you and find out more.

Regards,
Brett Millott
Principal
Glenroy West Primary School

Paul Kenna
Principal
Belle Vue Park Primary School

Brett and Paul came to visit Newcastle on several study trips. Paul wrote a strikingly useful email that includes many insights for the successful implementation of SOLEs:

April 7, 2011

Hi David, Sugata, Emma, Suneeta,

Great to read your email to Brett, David and a very interesting issue you have raised . . . how do teachers maintain a professional level of assessment whilst allowing space for students to also pursue their own learning. Our staff has just begun exploring this discussion . . . the dilemma of the content required by the department to be delivered and the flexibility for students to also pursue their own learning tangents.

Our staff currently develops "wonder walls" in each classroom where the focus of the content teachers are required to deliver is based on the inquiry approach . . . developing "provocations" for the students—asking a big question, with sub-content posed as further provocations. This allows for the system content to be delivered creatively and to enhance curiosity. We have moved away from planning centred on bland statements such as "The Zoo" and [toward] posing questions such as "Should animals have to live in cages?"

After some initial stimulus and conversations to provoke thought in the children, we begin the process of stimulating tangents of interest. The children are challenged to come up with their own questions and provocations. They can then follow these investigations and research in smaller groups. We have been working on grouping and classifying similar questions from the students and then forming some research groups where they can support each other in the research, discuss and learn together, and also develop their reports/presentations of their findings individually or in their groups.

The aspect of teachers being required to deliver the content but also allowing students the freedom to find things for themselves, follow their interest based on their own questions is interesting. Many times, it is fascinating to see where the students' interests take them, and where they go is sometimes surprising. If it were left to the teacher controlling the direction of the student learning, I am sure the enthusiasm, engagement, and learning direction aspect would be different.

I guess the "researching" aspect of students collaborating to find information and pursuing their "learning journey" is the tricky bit . . . building in the accountability. This year, we will be placing a

(Continued)

(Continued)

larger focus on the issue of setting more explicit learning intentions for students and providing clarity for students in the aspect of "success criteria" as it relates to their investigations.

Our Professional Learning Teams (groups of teachers who teach in the same level, for example Years 3 and 4) will do some action research in these areas. As a component of their performance review, they have been asked to develop three actions that they will implement to foster this inquiry process. They will also observe each other and provide feedback to each other (using a similar process to Instructional Rounds – Richard Elmore). The "engage" component of our E⁵ instructional model will also support staff in this focus . . . so really it does get back to developing the repertoire of teaching strategies and releasing some of that control that many teachers still feel is their duty to hold.

We might also utilise a capacity matrix to support the process and inform teachers on the process and the students on what their research should contain, which would support both "student freedom and curriculum accountability." For example,

Practices That Support Student Freedom and Curriculum Accountability
I tell my students what they are going to learn, rather than what they are going to do.
I explain to students what I'll be looking for to help me decide whether or not they have learned.
I use the learning intention and the success criteria as the basis for feedback to students.
I try to avoid grade-only feedback and tick-only feedback.
I include in my feedback to students recognition of what they have achieved and advice about how to improve.
I make use of "wait time" and "thinking time."
I make a point of asking open questions rather than closed questions.
I make use of the information I derive from questioning to shape my teaching and learning program.
I encourage peer feedback, based on the learning intention and success criteria, and provide opportunities for students to do this in a friendly and supportive environment.
I encourage students' self-assessment and self-evaluation and provide students with models and opportunities to develop these skills.

Cheers and all the best.

Regards,
Paul

Paul Kenna
Principal
Belle Vue Park Primary School

Paul's analysis was ahead of its time. It was about things that would happen around the world in a few years. His concerns and ideas about assessment would turn out to be the biggest of the challenges I would face. His observations about where children's own interests take them were uncanny. These would lead, one day, to my defining the teacher's role as "You go there; I will go with you."

By 2012, both principals were getting invited all over Australia and then to New Zealand to discuss their work. SOLEs began to spread in the great Down Under.

Argentina, Uruguay, and Chile

In 2005, the British Council of Argentina invited me to Buenos Aires for a lecture. It was my first visit to South America. I spoke to a large number of English teachers about how groups of children can learn to read and understand English if they have access to the internet and something interesting to do. It was a mistake to tell English teachers that the children could learn English on their own; however, I would make this mistake several times again, I am afraid.

On another visit to Argentina in 2010, I was invited by the University of Buenos Aires for a lecture and to visit several schools in the city and its suburbs. It was here that I conducted the first SOLE sessions in Spanish. Mabel Quiroga, a native of Argentina, translated, and the children and I had a whale of a time. It is here that I discovered that a SOLE would work in any language, provided there were enough online resources in that language.

Throughout 2010 to 2013, Latin America figured prominently in my life. Mabel and I visited Uruguay and conducted several experiments on reading comprehension with the One Laptop Per Child project (OLPC). Five years after OLPC, the children of Uruguay were reading better, it seemed, than children in most other countries. However, the curious thing is that whenever we gave a task to children that involved the internet, we would see them clustered around a computer in groups, even though everyone had a computer of her or his own. Once again, we saw evidence that comprehension happens in groups (Mitra & Quiroga, 2012).

In June of 2011, I was invited to Chile. I did several SOLE sessions in schools in Santiago. Of particular interest is one where we had no interpreter. I understood no Spanish (other than *baños*, I am afraid), and the children understood no English. We did the whole session using Google translate. It took a bit longer than usual, but it went just fine. Not only do teachers not need to know the answers to the questions they ask, they don't need to know the language the children speak! That's how much of a game changer the internet can be.

> **Not only do teachers not need to know the answers to the questions they ask, they don't need to know the language the children speak! That's how much of a game changer the internet can be.**

Back in Buenos Aires, Mabel took me to a school in a part of town where most of the children were pickpockets or petty criminals of some sort. I was to demonstrate a SOLE there. The class consisted of a group of 20 dour-faced 17-year-olds, looking bored and utterly disgusted at this intrusion from an odd-looking stranger.

I asked them why some of us had different colored hair. No response. Well, why do we have hair at all? There was a bit of giggling from the back. "Come on, tell me what's funny?" I pleaded.

"He is saying we don't have hair everywhere," said a girl and dissolved into giggles.

"Ah yes, why do we have hair in some places and not in other places—I have often wondered," I said, and Mabel translated with a severe expression. Now there was outright laughter.

"Do you want to figure it out on the internet? Will they let you use the internet in school?" I asked.

"Not for this kind of thing," said a boy with a huge Afro.

"Look, let's try anyway, for half an hour, and then you tell me what you think."

"There are only five computers in the room," said someone.

"I can't help that; you do what you can."

It took about ten minutes for the buzz of a SOLE to happen. More giggles.

"Most websites on the matter are blocked," said a student.

"OK," I said.

Half an hour later, the adolescents had almost forgotten us. They were deep in discussion about, you guessed it, sex. When the time came to report their views, it was a couple of girls who stood up. They spoke about thermal insulation, the loss of body hair for competitive hunting in savannahs, and the evolution of the ability to sweat.

"What about the other hair?" Mabel asked, after a prompting elbow jab from me.

The girls pointed at one of the boys and sat down. The room became silent.

We heard then about smell and the accumulation of glandular secretion for the purposes of identification and sexual attraction. The giggling had stopped.

"Fantastic!" I said, clapping.

As the session ended, the boys crowded around me, fist bumping and bowing. To me!

I knew my pocket would not be picked that day.

In my work with teenagers in SOLEs, I learned adolescents will engage with questions that are significantly different from the ones younger children find interesting. Adolescents like challenge, pragmatism, and rebellion. They like to challenge social norms and stigmas. SOLE facilitators need to create questions accordingly.

SOLEs started to spread all over Argentina, Chile, Uruguay, Brazil, Bolivia, Guatemala, and Mexico, and within many other countries I am sure I don't know about.

County Durham, England

Professor David Leat has been a director of the Research Centre for Learning and Teaching at Newcastle University for over 15 years. While I was stumbling about trying to understand self-organized learning, David was working on inquiry-based learning. We were both on the same track, and David instantly saw the pedagogical differences and began investigating SOLEs. He appointed Paul Dolan, a young assistant who would help me take SOLEs into schools in northeastern England.

North East England covers Northumberland, County Durham, Tyne and Wear, and the Tees Valley. The region has a rich industrial heritage. Plastics, nylons, petrochemicals, salt, glass, and other chemical industries were all located here in the past. It was the home of England's iron and steel and shipbuilding industries. And, of course, it was the center of the coal mining industry.

This region has a strong history in technological innovation: the friction match, steam locomotives, the incandescent light bulb, steam turbines, and hydraulics were all invented here. However, since the beginning of the twentieth century, the region has been in decline. As the industries disappeared from Britain, the northeastern part of the country was hit the hardest by the economic downturn.

Paul took me to schools all over County Durham during the summer of 2011. During the short train journeys, we evolved a method for introducing SOLEs into schools. We would start with a 30-minute lecture by me to the teachers. I would tell the story of the "Hole in the Wall," the little research studies, and the story of the experiments at St. Aidan's in Gateshead.

Then we would go into a classroom and conduct a SOLE with 8- to 12-year-olds, and with the teachers watching. I would not come "prepared." I would not know what question to ask. Instead, I would ask a teacher what she would have done in class if I had not come. Then I would make up a question that, hopefully, would get to the same learning outcomes. After the SOLE, we would go back to the staff room for a discussion. Sometimes, if there was time, we would ask one of the teachers to conduct a SOLE session while we watched. Then we would leave, hoping some of the teachers would try SOLEs by themselves. Almost universally, the teachers would adopt the method.

As we went from school to school, our confidence began to improve. The children reacted eagerly to SOLEs, once they understood they were really free and there was no "catch." Among many wonderful experiences, one stands out in my mind. The clean and beautiful primary school, which served disadvantaged children, was in a low-income area with a high rate of adult alcoholism.

"What were you going to teach if I had not come?" I asked the teacher. She said she was teaching British history.

"Have you covered the British Empire?" I asked. She looked a bit flustered.

"That's a bit embarrassing," she said. "We normally just touch upon it and move on to the world wars."

"Have you heard of the British Raj?" I asked the 9-year-olds. They shook their heads.

"Are you sure that is politically correct, Sugata?" asked the teacher a bit nervously.

"Don't worry," said Paul. "Just let him do his thing."

I explained what a SOLE was to the children. Let's see if we can get to an answer. This is an experiment. The children nodded vigorously; they liked experiments.

"What was the British Raj? Was it good or bad?"

"What's a 'raj'?" a child asked. I shrugged and shook my head.

The SOLE began with the usual chaos and noise. Groups formed and disintegrated. The teacher, Paul, and I moved to a corner of the room. We became invisible.

A group of four little girls were having an animated discussion. "Sugata, we have found the answer!" they said, after about 10 minutes.

"My goodness, that was quick!" I said. "So what is the answer?" The room was quiet.

"The British Raj is an Indian restaurant in South Shields [a nearby seaside town]," said one of the girls. "We are trying to find their menu online, to see if they are good or bad."

I gulped. Paul looked devastated. The teacher tried to keep a straight face. But there was commotion from another end of the room. A group of five boys, who, so far, seemed to specialize in moving around and irritating all the other groups, came up to the girls.

"It's not about restaurants, silly; it's about INDIA," they said, looking sideways at me. I tried to look as impassive as I could.

The girls took a look at the other group's screens. The SOLE became active again. It had self-corrected.

About 20 minutes later, I asked if anyone wanted to say something. One of the boys came up to the front of the room.

"The British Raj in India was both good and bad," he said, not looking at me. "The British did a lot of good things in India, but they did a lot of bad things too."

"Come on!" I said. "Don't give me a wishy-washy answer, please. Take a stance. Tell me was it good or was it bad—what's your opinion?"

"Can we have another 10 minutes?" asked the boy, looking to his friends for support. The SOLE restarted, this time with muted conversations and whispered arguments between groups.

"I am afraid, we are nearly out of time," I said, and the same boy as before came up. His voice was clear and precise.

"It was bad," he said. "The British did a lot of good things in India, but nobody asked them to."

I have never heard a better answer, I told them, applauding. Their teacher's eyes were wide with astonishment. Ever British, Paul said we needed some tea. The SOLE ended.

Since this experiment, I have seen numerous examples of SOLEs where errors of perception get corrected by the interaction of groups. SOLEs are self-correcting. Teachers and parents continue to be worried about how "the internet is full of rubbish" and how children may learn wrong ideas or concepts. I have not seen this happen, except when the conditions under which SOLEs are set up (interacting, unsupervised, self-organized groups) are not followed. This is a radical discovery. Imagine what would happen if adults didn't read opinion articles full of bias in the solitude of their own homes but rather in a group where they could self-correct each other. How would our society be different?

And yes, there are topics on which children can learn wrong ideas and concepts from the internet, such as religion and politics. Don't engage in SOLEs on these subjects if you are faint-hearted.

Days spent in SOLEs are filled with nervous anticipation, often ending in awe.

Did we really achieve anything? Well, many of the teachers went on to try SOLEs on their own. Word spread from staff room to staff room—SOLEs were cool.

My greatest reward was from an Ofsted report a year later—it was the second time after Australia that a government noticed the work. Ofsted is the Office for Standards in Education, Children's Services and Skills. It reports directly to the UK Parliament and is meant to be both independent and impartial. By law, it must inspect schools with the aim of providing information to parents in order to promote improvement and to hold schools to account. Schools have a love-hate relationship with Ofsted, and many a nervous joke is made about this office.

Here are some excerpts from an Ofsted report dated December 11, 2012:

> This example shows how an innovative approach to curriculum design at Middlestone Moor School has transformed the provision in core and foundation subjects. Standards are above average and rising as a result of pupils' excellent academic progress and very good personal development. Independent study skills, creative and formal writing skills, self-confidence and understanding of scientific enquiry are strong characteristics and begin from an early age. Social, moral, spiritual, and cultural aspects are carefully integrated into every topic.

It goes on to discuss the SOLE approach:

> Each topic also includes deliberate social, moral, cultural, and spiritual features that tackle pupils' personal development systematically and in context as part of subject-based learning. Teachers build in open-ended questions, using the examples suggested by the Self-Organised Learning Environment (SOLE) approach (pioneered by Professor Sugata Mitra of Newcastle University). For example, questions include: "What is the most amazing thing about the human body?"; "What kind of animals are endangered and why?"; "If the world is so beautiful, why are people worried about it?"; "Was the Raj good or bad?" Pupils are guided to answer for themselves, and learn how to organise research-based tasks. The questions are deliberately planned to be beyond pupils' current knowledge and understanding. (Ofsted, 2012, pp. 3–4)

Here was my reward, and a better reward is hard to come by.

Cambridge, Massachusetts, the United States

In December of 2010, I was surprised by an email from one of my heroes, Nicholas Negroponte, creator of MIT's fabled MediaLab in Cambridge, Massachusetts, and founder of the One Laptop Per Child (OLPC) initiative.

Sugata,

By chance, will you be in the USA, New York City or Boston, in the next month or two? I ask because I would enjoy meeting. I am more and more convinced that it is possible to do "learning without schools" at early ages, which is so important for the 100–200 million who have none. Few people agree.
      OLPC now has 2+ million laptops in the field, and I think we can prove it. Tablet coming soon. Love to talk to you about it. You are one of the few optimistic voices in the area of learning by yourself.

Hope this finds you well,
Nicholas

Nicholas wanted to find out if children could learn to read by themselves. He wanted to plan an experiment in Ethiopia. I met him on February 28, 2011, along with Cynthia Brezeal, the roboticist, and Maryanne Wolfe, the neuroscientist. We thought we had a plan.

What followed was this email, from March 4, 2011:

MIT can offer you a Visiting Professorship for two years without engaging in anything more than an internal Media Lab discussion. This would be paid and designed around your constraints, with or without Newcastle. What I need you to do is reflect on what would be the best for you and your family.

Why don't you and your wife discuss the conditions, financial and otherwise, that you would consider both fair and irresistible.

Irresistible, it certainly was!

I bought a tiny, fairy-tale cottage in Gateshead to store our things, and we moved to Cambridge, Massachusetts, in August 2011.

During the next 12 months, between Cambridge, Gateshead, and Calcutta, a lot happened. I wrote an e-book for TED (*Beyond the Hole in the Wall*) with a preface by Nicholas. I visited schools all over the United States and South America.

And then, in 2012–2013, I won the first ever million-dollar TED Prize.

"You go there; I will go with you."

Sugata Mitra

SCHOOLS IN THE CLOUD

TED: AN IDEA (I HOPE WAS) WORTH SPREADING

In February 2007, I was invited to speak at an event called LIFT (Leading Innovation for Tomorrow). Bruno Giussani, the European director of TED conferences, who was present, was so impressed with the talk, called *Kids Can Teach Themselves*, he obtained permission to upload it onto the TED website (see Video 2.1).

In July 2010, I gave a talk at TED Global in Oxford called *The Child-Driven Education* (see Video 2.2).

Video 2.1:
Kids Can Teach Themselves

Videos may also be accessed at **resources .corwin.com/ schoolinthecloud**.

Video 2.2:
The Child-Driven Education

Videos may also be accessed at **resources .corwin.com/ schoolinthecloud**.

While at Oxford, I had a mind-blowing experience—a talk about plant intelligence by Stefano Mancuso that changed me forever. That talk would later play into some of my SOLE sessions with children around the world, as you'll see later.

Back in the MIT Media Lab in Cambridge, MA, two Grannies had written to me, sharing the announcement for the TED Prize applications. Since it looked like an easy process, I wrote the few required paragraphs. My application proposed bringing together the cloud, schools, and children. Then, in October 2010, I received a call from Lara Stein, head of the first ever million-dollar TED Prize, letting me know that I had won! In November, after having moved back to Newcastle from Cambridge, I visited New York to present my plans for how I would use the prize money to Chris Anderson, the chief at TED. I said that I planned on building seven facilities for self-organized learning (five in India, two in the UK) and studying them for three years. We decided to call them "Schools in the Cloud."

That evening, back in my hotel near Canal Street, I had a funny experience. I was relaxed after a productive day, standing downstairs smoking a cigarette in the cool New York evening, when an elderly lady, a fellow smoker, joined me. It turned out she was visiting from England as well.

"What do you do?" she asked.

"I work with children's education at Newcastle University."

"Oh, I am a school teacher from Kent; so what about children's education?"

"Well, I am trying to figure out what the internet might do for children's education."

"Are you originally from India, if you don't mind my asking?"

"Not at all. Yes, I am from India, worked there most of my life."

"Oh my God! I have to tell you about this Indian guy—he put a computer in a wall for children, years ago. . . . Have you heard of him?"

"Sort of," I said. "Anyway, I really must go now."

I then walked rapidly away down Canal Street.

Video 2.3:
Build a School in the Cloud

Videos may also be accessed at **resources .corwin.com/ schoolinthecloud**.

In February 2013 in Long Beach, California, Sir Ken Robinson handed me the TED Prize on stage, where I gave a talk called *Build a School in the Cloud* (see Video 2.3).

Back in Calcutta, I put together a team to build the School in the Cloud, even though I didn't exactly know what I was doing. Ashis Biswas agreed to be the project manager. Ashis had decades of experience with computers, installations, facilities, marketing, and projects. Suneeta Kulkarni (an expert on child development and parenting) would be the research director. Ritu Dangwal (an expert on organizational psychology) would be the project coordinator. My wife, Sushmita (former director of Student Support Services for the Government of India), offered to help with administration. Her rather unenviable previous job was to look after the welfare of about half a million distance learners. Jerry Rothwell, filmmaker, was given an award by TED to film the entire project. You will see excerpts from his documentary, *The School in the Cloud* (2018), throughout Part II of this book.

THE SCHOOLS IN THE CLOUD

"My wish is to help design the future of learning by supporting children all over the world to tap into their innate sense of wonder. Help me build the School in the Cloud, a learning lab in India, where children can embark on intellectual adventures by engaging and connecting with information and mentoring online. I also invite you, wherever you are, to create your own miniature child-driven learning environments and share your discoveries."

Those were my words at the TED Long Beach event, when I accepted the prize from Sir Ken Robinson.

To plan the start of the School in the Cloud, we began with what we knew.

WHAT WE'VE LEARNED SO FAR (1999–2013)

- **Children are motivated to learn about topics that matter to them.** Children will independently seek information (other than examination subjects), advancing ten years ahead of the control group (their nonparticipating peers) within a few months. This possibility is unknown in conventional school settings.

- **Encouraging mentors boost performance.** In Kalikuppam (Southern India), Tamil-speaking children (ages 8 to 14 years) learned biotechnology on their own in English (to them, a foreign language). Their scores went from zero to 30 percent without the intervention of a teacher. With the introduction of a friendly and admiring mentor (Granny) who had no experience in teaching or biotechnology, the scores of these children increased from 30 percent to 51 percent. We observed similar growth among children in England using the SOLE method. In contrast, this model was tested in conventional classrooms in Hyderabad, but that yielded unfavorable results because the teachers would start to intervene, teach, and use authority.

- **Children can self-organize and learn in evolving groups.** Our most encouraging finding was that children can self-organize and learn in evolving groups, all by themselves, when appropriate resources are provided. This result is reproducible and has been supported by data.

- **SOLEs level the playing field.** The positive indications are overwhelming. They inspire not only us but also educators and innovative thinkers around the world, including the folks at TED. An Australian school principal who uses SOLEs regularly commented, "All SOLEs look alike, no matter where on the planet they are conducted." We saw the potential for this project to provide a level playing field for all children all over the world. We also knew that, in order for it to gain traction, it needed to be a grassroots effort, growing from the bottom upward.

- **SOLEs have a huge appeal among some teachers.** Teachers around the world reported that they were doing SOLEs—blogging about it and posting videos of SOLEs on YouTube.

- **There are indicators that SOLEs have long-lasting effects.** Two independent teachers have said that children are reading ahead of their time. In one school, Year 3 and Year 4 did SOLEs for two years, after which they discontinued the practice for various reasons. The two groups exposed to SOLEs are reported as reading better than other groups.

THE CHALLENGES OF SOLES

- **Equipment maintenance and technical issues.**

- **Contested use of space.** Resistance came from schools that thought the space and equipment could be better used for more "important" things. At one such school in India, the principal suggested that the SOLE would be better used as a cowshed—and that's eventually what it became. We called this the "cowshed effect."

- **Cultural obstacles.** We observed that parents and teachers, due to mindsets and conventional thinking, never paid much attention to the children's ability to self-organize. Parents were satisfied that their children were going to school, and it did not matter what happened when they got there. The objective of the project was thus deterred by the resistance and/or ignorance of the society and conventional systems.

- **Systemic pedagogical constraints.** Although teachers in England are well equipped and understand the concept of SOLE, many SOLE teachers conduct SOLEs very intermittently due to impending tests and examinations. Teachers hate teaching to the test, but they often have to.

- **Incorrect implementation.** Many inspired teachers devised their own method of conducting SOLEs—with little success. Unfortunately, they reported that the method does not work, but they were not implementing it correctly.

- **Standardized instructional materials were needed.** We needed to develop training material. Thus far, I had been doing full demonstrations as well as interacting with teachers to clarify their understanding. This was clearly not sustainable to promote the project at its new scale.

- **Support.** We need to develop more ambassadors, such as our friends Brett and Paul in Australia.

- **Sustainability.** Could we develop a sustainable funding model that would enable the schools to continue to flourish once we depleted the TED funding? This question continues to be a central concern, as you will see throughout the remainder of this book.

- **Ultimate impact.** Finally, we wondered about the ultimate impact of the project. We knew that children who participated in SOLEs could pass exams, but we wondered whether they were just memorizing information. We also considered whether their test scores were good enough when compared to those educated using other methods. Would SOLEs encourage better and long-lasting learning?

You may wonder why English features so prominently in these questions about language acquisition. It would need another book to explain that! In India, people who know English well have an incredible advantage over people who don't.

Two research questions guided our inquiry:

Q1: Can groups of children, when provided with the appropriate equipment and space, understand, speak, and have sufficient reading comprehension skills to use the internet (for searching) without the help of a physical teacher?

Q2: Is it possible for groups of children to speak and understand English and adopt the associated manners and etiquettes without the help of a physical teacher?

We started with choosing the locations for the seven sites, which we called areas. The locations were based on three socioeconomic strata.

Bottom of the socioeconomic ladder

- Area 0 (Gocharan, West Bengal): This is near Calcutta and is a semi-urban location with schools nearby.

- Area 1 (Korakati, West Bengal): This is our remotest area in the Sundarbans delta of the Ganges. It has no electricity or water supply. It has nearly no healthcare or schools.

- Area 2 (Chandrakona, West Bengal): This is a village about 100 kilometers from Calcutta. It is a rural, farming area. But it is neither as poor nor as remote as Korakati.

Middle of the socioeconomic ladder

- Area 3 (Kalkaji, New Delhi): The location was a government school in a slum of New Delhi. The area is urban but very poor.

- Area 4: (Phaltan, 257 km south of Mumbai): The location was a school in the town of Phaltan serving the urban middle class, but some of the students came from neighboring rural areas. About 30% had tuition fee waivers.

Upper end of the socioeconomic ladder

- Area 5 (Killingworth, North East England): Killingworth is a suburb of Newcastle upon Tyne, an urban, middle-class area of Britain. The facility is inside the George Stephenson High School.

- Area 6 (Newton Aycliffe, North East England): The facility is inside a community center and a school in a semi-urban area.

The program goal was for children to self-organize and evolve in order to challenge their own abilities and talents. Our intention was merely to provide the technology and access they needed in order to self-organize and learn—if indeed they chose to do so, as they always do. There cannot be any special teaching method for that. No pedagogy is good pedagogy.

> If a group of children can search the internet, read, and understand what they find (most of the internet is in English), and have a reason to do all this—the rest of learning seems to take care of itself.

This observation has been described as naïve, simplistic, harmful, wrong, and so on, mostly by people who have not tried it. Teachers who have tried it, and there are thousands of them worldwide, can see where I am coming from but may be confused by where all this might go.

Figure 2.1 The Seven Sites of the SOLE Locations

Source: Map data ©2019 Google, ORION-ME

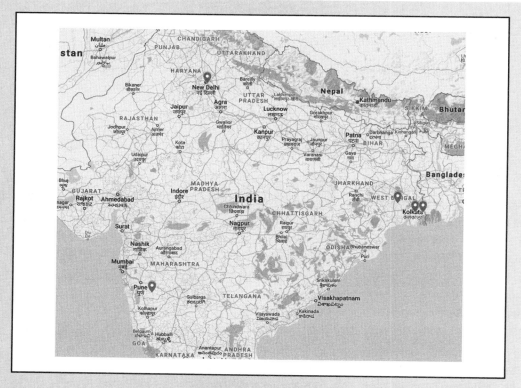

Figure 2.2 Areas 0–4, India

Source: Map data ©2019 Google

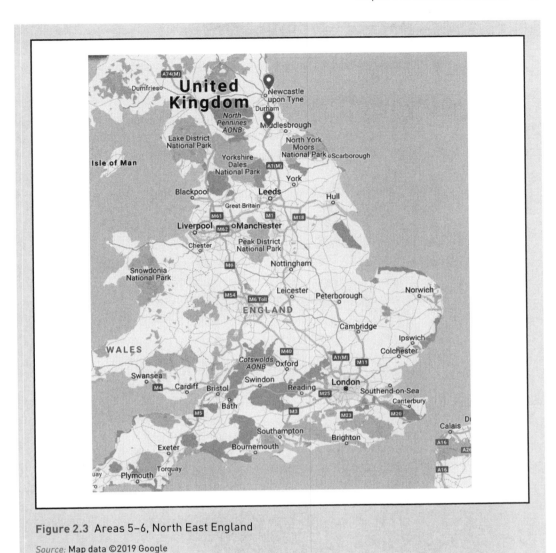

Figure 2.3 Areas 5–6, North East England

Source: Map data ©2019 Google

To measure the impact of the School in the Cloud (shortened to "SinC"—a rather unfortunate nickname, but it stuck), we decided to measure English reading comprehension, aspirations, and the ability to use the internet.

Reading Fluency and Comprehension (RFC)

These were the most important areas of our assessment. The testing was done only in India. Much of this testing was not really relevant to the UK where the children were fluent in English. We used three ways to measure RFC.

1. A basic screening tool (ASER)

2. Graded reading passages (Super Teacher worksheets)

3. Qualitative data related to RFC as judged through search activities engaged in by the children.

In India, we first established a baseline by testing a random sample of children at each site. Then we tested them each month for about three years.

To introduce the ASER tests that we used, I will tell you a bit about Pratham, an innovative learning organization in India (Banerjee & Duflo, 2011; Pratham, 2019). Pratham provides quality education to underprivileged children (see Pratham India Education Initiative, 2009). In 2005, Pratham launched a massive survey of primary education in India and published the results in a report called ASER (Annual Status of Education Report). We decided to use the ASER reading task because this tool was developed by Pratham for a basic assessment of reading abilities, in English, across the Indian subcontinent, particularly in rural areas. Using the ASER task can facilitate a comparison of children's reading fluency across groups of children from within the Schools in the Cloud or between these children's scores and the national reading level. In conjunction with ASER, our assessments involved a few additional tasks to allow for the assessment of reading comprehension in addition to reading fluency. We decided to do this based on our observations that fluency does not necessarily correlate with comprehension.

At this stage, we looked for the following:

Fluency—accuracy (including self-correction), pausing (punctuation), rate (pace of reading), and expression (indication of comprehension of meaning through, for example, intonation or stress and emphasis). We were looking for comprehension, not elocution.

Comprehension—identification of the key elements, essence, or main idea of the passage; summarization of ideas or key events in chronological sequence; comprehension of the meanings of key words and terms (manifested in translation); and manifestation of an understanding of the passage's context (e.g., its title, author, theme, or connection to other information or knowledge).

The Aspirations Tool

We wanted to check whether children exposed to the "wider" world would want to be different from what they were. Would children's aspirations (what they want to be or become) undergo a change either in terms of becoming higher or being toned down with realism or becoming more varied based on their experiences in the School in the Cloud?

We asked children in Grade 5 and above these questions:

1) What would you like to become?

2) What preparation do you need to do this?

3) Do you have a role model for this aspiration? If so, who is it?

The questions were translated, if necessary, into the local language. The children were asked the questions when the labs first opened in December 2014 or January 2015 and then again toward the end of the project (July through October 2016).

Self-Confidence Observations

We defined confidence as "a belief in one's ability to achieve an objective." Children in traditional school settings can be anxious and apprehensive. There is a large body of work on this (see, for example, McDonald, 2001). Would the School in the Cloud alter these emotions? Would an increased confidence in their abilities affect their capability to learn? We hoped so.

At the beginning of the program, we assessed children's confidence levels on a five-point scale based on this statement: *This child is high on confidence.* The scoring options were as follows: Strongly Agree (5); Agree (4); Undecided (3); Disagree (2); Strongly Disagree (1). The observer was guided by a list of the indicators to be observed before awarding the final score. We assumed that these qualities would not be different between England and India, particularly for the age groups we were dealing with.

The indicators on the self-confidence observation sheet were as follows:

- Expresses his or her thoughts

- Responds freely to questions without worrying about whether or not his or her answer is "correct" (traditionally, this is not encouraged in England or India)

- Comments on activity

- Asks for specific activities (stories, songs, puzzles)

- Speaks without being prompted

- Directs activity from behind, "for example", pointing to where something needs to be accessed on the screen

- Shares his or her work

- Does not give up easily, even when the task is difficult

- Explores in different ways, using different strategies

- Takes responsibility for tasks on his or her own initiative

- Takes responsibility for tasks assigned to him or her

- Directs activity

- Asks and gives help when required

Search Skills

I developed a tool, called "TBT4KA," to gauge children's responses to "big questions." These questions we graded from those needing answers that are purely factual to those needing considered answers based on facts and reasoning and, ultimately, to those that do not have a single answer or any answer at all. The test would measure the effectiveness with which SOLE students used internet resources to arrive at their conclusions.

TBT4KA: A Task-Based Test for Knowledge Acquisition From the Internet

"I don't need to know everything; I just need to know where to find it, when I need it."

These words, which are commonly attributed to Einstein, were written decades before the internet was created. They are prophetic. They predict an age when "knowing" becomes obsolete. We live in that age.

This does not mean we don't need to know things. We do. It's just that we don't need to know as much as possible in the first seventeen years of our lives—and then remember and use this knowledge for the rest of our lives.

There was once a time when, in most situations, if we needed to use knowledge, we had to get it from our own memory. That world does not exist anymore. When we need to know, we can know in seconds, provided we have access to the internet.

In this world, we need the skills to access the knowledge we need. We need to know where and how to find knowledge. These are very different skills than the skills needed to access information in a library.

The TBT4KA test was developed to measure whether or not children have acquired the skills to learn things rapidly, accurately, and confidently. It is designed to measure whether children, either individually or in groups, can answer questions and solve problems using the information "cloud" and the myriad of access techniques and devices that pervade our world today.

> **We need the skills to access the knowledge we need.**

We designed questions of different levels of complexity from Level 1 to Level 6. They ranged from purely factual questions to those that require critical thinking. For example, a Level 1 question might be "What time is it in New York?" while a higher level question might be "Why do things float or sink?" As the levels increase, the complexity of the answers also increases, as questions become more abstract and, sometimes, have no *one* right answer. The scoring of answers is based on three parameters: an answer's "appropriateness" (relevance to the question asked), its "quality," and the "time taken" to find the answer. Each level has four equivalent questions. Such a test measures searching, reading, technological literacy, and analysis skills all at once. We don't have a name yet for this "all-in-one" skill. It is a new kind of literacy.

The test is scored by independent experts who rate answers based on the three parameters. Additionally, there are subparameters such as (a) depth of coverage, (b) clarity of content, (c) originality (has the child taken material from other sites or expressed the answer in his or her own words), and (d) coherence. Tests can be administered to groups or individually. We recommend first administering the test to groups to build confidence. As the children progress to higher levels, the test can be administered individually. We recommend administering the test three times a year.

It is assumed that if a child is able to answer a question, she or he has acquired basic operational skills such as the following: opening a browser and using a search engine, identifying hyperlinks, clicking on a hyperlink and opening a new window, closing a tab, juggling between multiple windows, going forward and backward using a browser, and exploring websites by scrolling up and down.

The highest level of comprehension can be measured by a child's ability to answer Level 6 questions. Since Level 6 questions do not necessarily have a right or wrong answer, to access whether a child is parroting someone else's opinion rather than her or his own, we rely on other children to correct group members, cross reference, and verify. We know from our previous experience in SOLE settings that children are seldom fooled.

I've provided an example of the TBT4KA test here (Figure 2.4), with samples of the kinds of questions that might be included, so that you can try it out in your own classes.

Procedure:

Step 1: Label each group (Group 1, Group 2, etc.) and record the names of the children in the group.

Step 2: Pick any question from Level 1 for the group or child to answer.

The teacher says to students, "Here is a question. You can sit in groups and find the answer. You can talk to each other but not to other groups. There is no time limit. When you finish, hand over your answer to me. If you find any question too difficult and are unable to answer, you have reached the end of the test."

Step 3: Record how many minutes it takes for the group or child to come up with an answer.

Step 4: Repeat the process for Level 2 and so on until the group or child is unable to answer satisfactorily or has reached the last level.

(Continued)

(Continued)

List of Questions

Level 1: Simple, factual, and usually with one "right" answer

- What time is it in New York?
- What is the temperature in Cape Town?
- What is the distance from the Earth to the Moon?
- How much do elephants weigh?
- What do owls eat?
- What is Egypt famous for?
- Who was Victor Hugo?
- Where is Easter Island?

Level 2: Simple but with possible ambiguity regarding what is the "right" answer

1. Who invented the telephone?
2. Which is the longest river in the world?
3. Which is the biggest animal in the world?
4. Which is the smallest bird in the world?
5. Which is the tallest mountain in the world?
6. Which is the smallest country in the world?
7. Can a tiger swim?
8. Who painted Mona Lisa?

Level 3: Facts that require thinking and assimilation of some other knowledge

1. Why are there no dinosaurs today?
2. Why does the Earth go around the Sun?
3. What are drums made of?
4. Why does hot water cool down?
5. Why is a polar bear white?
6. What is a tornado?
7. Can fish sneeze?
8. What is wool made of?

Level 4: Ambiguous, with multiple answers possible

1. Is there life on other planets?
2. How are pencils made?

3. Why is a giraffe's neck so long?

4. What is a rainbow made of?

5. Why do we cough when we have a cold?

6. Why does hair on our heads grow?

7. Why do we have to eat and drink?

8. How is cloth made?

Level 5: Complex answers based on theory or multiple theories

1. Where did language come from?

2. When did the world begin? When and how will it end?

3. Can trees think?

4. Why does water boil when heated?

5. Why is seawater salty?

6. Why do we have to sleep?

7. Why do people smile when they are happy?

8. What is electricity?

Level 6: Complex or unknown answers that require considered opinion

1. Why are women (usually) shorter than men?

2. Why do we have five fingers and toes? Why not another number?

3. Will robots replace human beings?

4. What is infinity?

5. How do we remember? Why do we forget?

6. What is the purpose of theater and drama?

7. How does a mobile phone send our voice from one phone to another?

8. Why do children lose their teeth and grow a new set?

Figure 2.4 Assessment Instrument for Children's Development of Search Skills

NB: The assessor should fill out a form for each group of children being tested, numbering the group in the spot indicated in #3.

1. **Class/School/Site:** _____

2. **Date of Administration:** _____

3. **Names and ages of children in Group #_____ :**

   i. _____ age: _____ M/F

   ii. _____ age: _____ M/F

   iii. _____ age: _____ M/F

   iv. _____ age: _____ M/F

   v. _____ age: _____ M/F

Question 1.

Answer 1.

[Time taken to answer the question]

Question 2.

Answer 2.

[Time taken to answer the question]

Question 3.

Answer 3.

[Time taken to answer the question]

Question 4.

Answer 4.

[Time taken to answer the question]

Question 5.

Answer 5.

[Time taken to answer the question]

Question 6.

Answer 6.

[Time taken to answer the question]

Figure 2.5 Assessment Data Sheet: Development of Search Skills

Suneeta was apprehensive because the test had not been validated. It would take years to develop it into a calibrated and trustworthy instrument. I decided to use the test as it was, anyway. Based on our earlier Hole-in-the-Wall experiments, we knew that children's ability to find answers increased in a School in the Cloud, but we did not know how. We hoped that this test might provide us with some insights.

In Chapter 4 you will find graphs that show the growth in searching skills among the children in the program. While the instrument is not calibrated (unlike those for reading comprehension), we can nonetheless verify growth.

The searching skills test is highly subjective. The questions that form each level are created simply from my observation of children doing SOLEs in various countries and what they find easy or difficult. Similarly, the scoring of the answers, particularly for the more conceptual questions at Level 4 and higher, is purely subjective. Although the scoring is subjective, we found a 90 percent rate of inter-rater reliability.

It is worth pointing out that assessments in the SinC labs take place in far from ideal conditions. Certain things cannot be controlled, such as the number of children in the room, the noise level, interruptions and distractions, internet speeds or malfunctions, the level of prior knowledge children bring, a child's tenure in the program, a child's choice of group, or a child's irregular attendance. Nonetheless, expert researchers did their level best to administer assessments in a scientifically sound way and to analyze data as conscientiously as possible, but drawing conclusions or correlating presence in the lab with the improvements children make is still uncertain territory.

In Part II of this book, I will introduce you to the seven areas where we tested children's abilities to learn on their own.

Suneeta put all this together, and then she and Ritu went into the field.

SCHOOLS IN
THE CLOUD

AREA ZERO: GOCHARAN, THE BARUIPUR MUNICIPALITY, BENGAL, INDIA

On the highway joining the cities of Baruipur and Joynagar in the southern suburbs of Calcutta is a tiny semi-urban, literate village called Gocharan. Large amounts of the land of Gocharan belong to twin sisters—Mala and Dola. Mala gave us a sizable plot of land between two ponds to build a School in the Cloud. This would be the flagship of the TED project, the largest School in the Cloud.

The School in the Cloud in Gocharan consists of two concentric hexagons. By joining the faces of the two hexagons with imaginary lines, you can visualize six

Figure 3.1 The Gocharan Site Before the School in the Cloud Was Built

spaces. If one of the spaces is used as a reception and administration area, we are left with five areas, each with two computers. Ten computers with four children on each would give us a capacity of 40 children at a time. The central hexagon would have a large screen for Skype sessions. Behind the structure would be a guest room with a bathroom. Adjoining the computer room would be two bathrooms one for boys and one for girls.

I chose the hexagon as the basic shape for two reasons, both more symbolic than dictated by engineering. The hexagon is the shape formed by six carbon atoms in organic compounds. This shape forms the building block for all life as we know it. The hexagon is also the shape of all cells in a beehive. It is the most economical use of space. Carbon hexagons and beehive hexagons are both emergent phenomena, order out of chaos. I liked that.

Area Zero, Gocharan, was inaugurated on January 9, 2014. It was a magnificent structure, much bigger than all the others. Ashis Biswas, the project manager, had to modify my plan because of the land layout and architectural reasons, and the resultant structure was glorious—and very expensive to build, at £86,000 (USD 130,000 or INR 8,600,000, approximately). That was more than 10 percent of the TED Prize money.

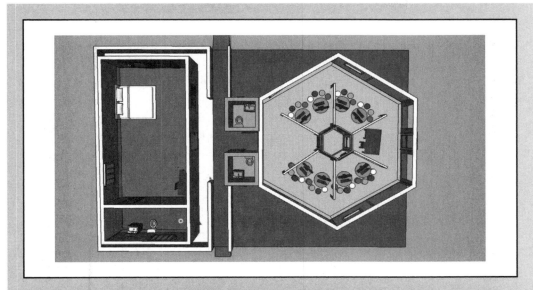

Figure 3.2 The Original Design for the School in the Cloud at Gocharan

Source: Created using SketchUp, ©2019 Trimble Inc.

Figure 3.3 The School in the Cloud at Gocharan

In my original design, the roof was to be flat, but Ashis thought it would look better if it were a six-sided cone, and indeed it did. We had put in solar power, even though the area has good public electricity. The Gocharan opening was covered by the global media.

Local parents whom I spoke to on the day of inauguration were curious and delighted to see the facility. The children were also excited. Gathering a sample of students, Suneeta measured baseline reading comprehension, confidence, and internet searching abilities. Many of the children had experienced internet access through their parents' phones, but their reading comprehension levels were poor.

LEARNING AND SOME HUGE CHALLENGES

At the Gocharan site, the children visited in batches of 40, clustering around eight computers. This large number of students resulted in several problems.

- There were too many groups, leading to too much movement across the space. Coherent discussion was impossible.

- Self-organization, when it occasionally happened in pockets, was brief and often interrupted by others.

- The Granny sessions were held inside the inner hexagon. There was no way that more than 10 children could all fit into that space. As a result, the ones who were left out (about 20 to 40 at a time) continued to play and make a lot of noise.

- The glass walls and the conical roof produced loud echoes. With eight computers playing eight different YouTube videos, it was sometimes impossible to converse or hear anything at all. It became impossible to conduct Granny sessions in the inner hexagon. It was bedlam.

Ashis reduced some of the noise by putting sheets of jute on the sides of the conical roof, but it continued to be very loud inside. It turns out that the conical roof was a bad idea.

Shoumen Maitra, Mala's husband, had started out by charging the parents a monthly fee for sending their children. Within months, attendance started to drop as parents noticed the crowds of children, the absence of "teachers," and the noisy Granny sessions that only four to six children could participate in. Gocharan proved to be an example of a cohort that was too large, resulting in too much noise to self-organize or produce emergent behavior.

RESULTS

Suneeta could not assess a core sample of children consistently because children would not attend consistently on set days of the week. She therefore began to rely more on case studies. But even these were not consistent enough to form any general conclusions. However, like the Hole-in-the-Wall experiment of 1999, we did observe individual cases of high achievement. The vignette that follows is an excerpt from one of Suneeta's case studies and published in the Granny Cloud Tales blog.

CASE STUDY: GOCHARAN

Deb is an obviously bright, intelligent, healthy young boy who started using the SinC lab at Gocharan when it opened in 2014. He was then 13 years old and in Grade 8. Deb is among the older children at the lab. He attends the local school, which is a Bengali medium school.

Deb comes from a very poor family. He lives with his parents and younger sister, Titly, in an old, mildewed ancestral home just a few minutes away from the SOLE lab. His mother is a homemaker who does odd craft jobs in her spare time to supplement the family income. The parents would like him to have a life different from their own, and put in a great deal of effort to ensure they can provide all that they think he needs.

His mother's vision of his future is limited in a very loving way, and her involvement in his life focuses on feeding him properly and ensuring he is rested. In terms of his achievements, she is concerned that he should give more weight to his books and studies and tuitions (private tutoring sessions), which Deb attends without fail. She has a hard time understanding how his "playing" at the lab will feed into his career, though she doesn't interfere because she sees his joy and instinctively realizes it must have some impact. Like many other parents, she finds his interaction with the grannies to be a boon. She thinks he doesn't spend enough time studying, not realizing that he grasps at one reading what it takes many other children several readings to understand. His father is proud of him and enjoys a game of cricket with him too. He has installed a practice ball for him in the veranda, which also doubles as a living room, so Deb can "bat away."

Access to the Lab

Deb lives next door to the lab, which makes it easy for him to attend frequently. He tends to pass it on his way to anywhere, and he checks to see if it is open, even at odd times. His age also made it easier for him to be independent as he was not dependent on his parents bringing him to the lab.

Reading Fluency and Comprehension

Deb's beginning scores during the baseline assessment in January 2015 on the ASER already placed him in the "eligible to proceed to the next level of RFC tasks" He scored 100 percent for fluency as well as comprehension.

Deb was assessed again in March 2015, using the Level 2 RFC task, which was a graded worksheet. He handled this worksheet competently, including reading at an appropriate pace, with punctuation and expression. He indicated comprehension through his ability to translate into his mother tongue, sentence by sentence, word by word as part of the comprehension task. He was able to do the same even for a reading task at the middle school (Grade 7) level, although this required slightly more effort and his pronunciation reflected the local accent for specific words.

During the final RFC assessment in July 2016, Deb was assessed using reading tasks at two levels. The first was a reading passage at the middle school (Grade 6) level; it consisted of many unfamiliar words (e.g., "marsupial"). Deb's reading style showed a marked difference from his start point. His voice was softer, and he no longer read in the "elocution style" that dominated his reading in the initial

(Continued)

(Continued)

assessment. While the local accent was still in evidence, it was not intrusive. As this was a relatively hard task, Deb read the passage aloud by following each word with his finger. He was undeterred by unfamiliar words and figured them out. He was able to explain in his mother tongue (Bengali) the meaning of the passage, although the influence of school expectations was still evident in his persever-ance in explaining every sentence, rather than providing a summary of the text, as had been asked for.

The second task we assessed Deb on was reading a printed news item. This posed difficulty in terms of unfamiliar words as well as in terms of the small font size. Deb read this item also by following each word with his finger. He guessed at pronunciations of unfamiliar words (e.g., proper nouns such as "Gaglione" and "mimosa"), and he also showed evidence of self-correction. His reading speed varied: picking up when he came across sentences containing words he knew and slowing down when the words were unknown. He was able to comprehend at this level as well, and he provided an explana-tion in both English (in his own words) and Bengali. He was able to provide the gist of the passage to a greater extent when speaking in Bengali. The influence of the mother tongue was evident in his mixing genders and attributing gender to plants.

Aspirations

Like many other children, Deb had indicated wanting to be a teacher when he grows up when he was questioned about this during the initial assessments. His mathematics teacher was his role model. The access to a wider world was evident in his responses in August 2016. He indicated wanting to be either a computer programmer, which connects directly to an interest that he developed and pursued during his 16 months at the SinC lab, or a cricketer, an interest he shares with his father and now knows much more about!

Strategies: Approach to Using the SOLE Lab

Deb is interested in many different things, from computers and programming to science to cricket and wrestling. He chose to be present for Granny sessions even if it meant he was the only one interacting with a Granny (given that, at Gocharan, Granny sessions were not terribly popular because of the noise levels and added difficulties in interacting).

He takes a lot of initiative, and he had a fair amount of starting confidence, which went up even fur-ther. He is patient, waits his turn, and watches what the others do (as opposed to being impulsive). He is also helpful, has a sense of responsibility, and has varied interests rather than being interested only in schoolwork. He uses the lab for both fun and work. Deb recognizes the opportunities this provides and ensures that he asks for help, even from younger children, while also providing support himself, even to the youngest ones in the lab.

Deb spends his time in the lab playing games and watching videos, just as much as exploring and developing a skill. Searching for answers to "big questions" set by a coordinator or doing tasks he has set himself appeals to him. From time to time, he likes to work alone so that he can hone a skill or pursue his thought process in a concentrated manner. For this, he often makes the most of time when there are fewer children in the lab, and he can have access to a computer on his own. At other times, he prefers to sit in a group, usually with a more or less fixed set of children of different ages with whom he has shared interests.

He participates in village activities including the village library, taking responsibility for gathering reading material and otherwise keeping it going. He can be serious about things but knows how to have fun and is also involved in pranks and light-hearted teasing. He is respectful of adults even when they don't warrant it. He explores as much as he can, making the most of the facilities offered to him through the lab. Unlike some of his friends who come from wealthier families, Deb recognizes the need to make the most of whatever resources are available to him.

Special Achievements

Among the typical characteristics of "successful" children in the SinC labs is the ability to make the most of opportunities.

In Deb's case, this was particularly evident in his interaction with the grannies, particularly Fabio from Brazil, who engaged with him one on one and taught him the rudiments of programming, and Rodger from Australia, who provided some general encouragement. With their support, Deb was able to develop a "chatbot" and a Tetris-like game, and he has continued to develop his programming skills in the couple of months since the project ended. Deb has probably interacted with almost every single Granny who has Skyped into Gocharan and explored many different issues along with a group of enthusiastic boys, as well as through individual interaction with them, even when other children did not wish to do so.

I interacted with Deb's bot. It was written in JavaScript.

Bot: What is your name?

Sugata: Sugata

Bot: Where do you live?

Sugata: Calcutta. Where do you live?

Bot: I live in this computer in a School in the Cloud.

Not bad for a village boy from Bengal, teaching himself programming with the help of a Brazilian and an Australian. If that isn't a glimpse of the future of learning, I don't know what is.

Some fathers grudgingly admit that their children have learned a lot about computers and the internet. Mothers know it must be beneficial based on how much their children love attending. However, mothers worry whether these skills will help their children get into university and succeed in a career.

To me, Gocharan is an example of how *not* to design a School in the Cloud.

The School in the Cloud in Gocharan remained open until the TED Prize funding ran out in November 2018. Shoumen says the facility is not financially viable. He is considering converting it into a computer school with teachers.

Bengal is staunchly Victorian in its view of education, school, and "schooling." Bengal is still in the early twentieth century.

The School in the Cloud will have to struggle to survive in this ancient world.

AREA 1: KORAKATI, THE SUNDARBANS, BENGAL, INDIA

Nitish Mondol teaches Bengali in a government school in Calcutta, and he is featured extensively in the documentary film *The School in the Cloud*. He is from a village called Korakati, in the Sundarbans. "Sundarban" (in Bengali) translates to "beautiful forest." The Sundarbans is a vast forest in the coastal region of the Bay of Bengal; considered one of the natural wonders of the world, it was recognized in 1997 as a UNESCO World Heritage Site. It is the world's largest coastal mangrove forest, containing numerous species of animals, birds, and reptiles, including the Bengal tiger, chital deer, crocodiles, and snakes.

Korakati has no electricity, sanitation, sewerage, clean water, health care, or schools (to speak of). In March of 2013, Nitish showed up unannounced at the gate of my house in a suburb of Calcutta one morning before I had gotten out bed. He wanted a School in the Cloud. He did not know what it was and had only read about my TED Prize in a local Bengali newspaper.

"Whatever you do will be good," Nitish said, with firm conviction.

Intrigued, I dispatched Ashis to Korakati.

"It's impossible to do anything in that place; there is nothing there," he reported wearily.

"Then we have to build our School in the Cloud there," I said.

To get to Korakati, we drove two hours to the port village of Dhamakhali. Then, we took a boat. The boats are small and narrow, powered by a lawn-mower motor. Sometimes, a hundred people ride on a single boat. These boats sink often, washing people away. The boat ride lasts about 30 minutes. From the port village of Mathura Bazar, we take a "van." This is made of half a motorcycle, usually a Royal Enfield left by the British after World War II. The front half of the motorcycle is attached to a wooden platform that has four bicycle wheels. People sit all around this platform, their legs dangling. We call these vehicles "bone shakers." Korakati is an hour's ride on a boneshaker from Mathura Bazar. The roads are just wide enough for the van. En route, passengers use their legs to push aside goats, cattle, and ducks. On either side are lush green rice paddies and ponds. Idyllic, if you are not shaking too much, but lethal if you fall into one. The beautiful ponds contain bacteria and viruses, many of them deadly.

Figure 4.1 The Korakati Site Before the School in the Cloud Was Built

Figure 4.2 The School in the Cloud at Korakati

Watch Video 4.1 Korakati. In this video excerpt from Rothwell's *The School in the Cloud* (2018), you can hear villagers from Korakati talk about their hopes for the yet to be build School in the Cloud.

The structure at Korakati is a large rectangular space with a veranda surrounding it on all sides. The space inside contains one room for batteries, two guest rooms with bathrooms, and two toilets for children. The main space contains six computers with 19-inch screens and a large smart TV for live Skype connections. All the walls are mostly glass. There is an air conditioner in the main space. There is a water tank on the roof with a small pump that fills it up from a well at ground level. Solar panels charge a bank of batteries that provide electricity. On a sunny day, it takes about an hour to charge the batteries fully. Most days are sunny in Korakati, which means we can run the air conditioner for about 45 minutes with a gap of an hour after each run. However, it is seldom used, for a bittersweet reason.

Ashis accomplished the impossible by building the School in the Cloud in Korakati in just under six months. It was inaugurated on March 9, 2014, when the cement was still a bit wet. Ashis managed to get a wireless internet connection by raising a receiver about 40 feet off the ground using bamboo poles. The signal was from the government telecom company, BSNL, and came from about 10 miles away—from an island called Sandeshkhali.

On the day of the inauguration, we had the air conditioner on as it was a balmy 32°C (89.6°F). I was outside, watching the children through the glass walls. They were engrossed trying to figure the computers out. After about half an hour, a little girl in a sleeveless frock ran out.

Video 4.1: Korakati

Videos may also be accessed at **resources .corwin.com/ schoolinthecloud**.

"What happened?" I asked.

"So lovely and warm outside!" she said, hugging herself. The bodies of these children were acclimatized to feel comfortable only at temperatures ranging from 30–40°C (86–104°F) and at humidity levels of 75 percent and over. So much for my air conditioner.

On the day of the inauguration, one of the Cloud Grannies came online, to a tumultuous welcome from the children. She began by singing "The Wheels of the Bus Go Round and Round." The children looked puzzled, and the Granny insisted, "Now say it again . . . the wheels of the bus. . . ."

"What else can the wheels of a bus do?" muttered a little girl in Bengali. I tried not to smile and to be as minimally invasive as possible. Such were the cultural differences we were blessed to work with.

We opened the facility around 9 a.m. every day, in bright daylight, and closed it before sunset. Parents don't like to send or bring their children when it is dark and misty.

There are six computers in Korakati, and the room can hold about 24 children at a time. We let in the first 24 who arrived and asked the others to wait outside. The weather and the verandas make this waiting area quite comfortable. After an hour, we let the children know that their turn was over, and then we let in the next 24 children.

Inside, the children played games, looked at YouTube videos (Charlie Chaplin is a favorite, bless his soul), and, in a few weeks, started to search for things. Grannies would visit via Skype about once a week for an hour or so and, sometimes, leave a question for the children to answer. Children would discuss the Granny Cloud sessions with each other all the time, and even the ones who were not present during the Granny session would know what happened and join in the search for information.

In less than a month, the children began to speak in English when they wanted to. "Take care," said a little girl, when I was leaving after a visit.

"Thank you! How on earth did you learn to speak in English?" I asked in Bengali.

She grinned and replied in Bengali, "That Granny who comes on the screen, she can't understand anything else other than English. So what can we do?"

About four months into the experiment, the internet at Korakati failed. Our signal was coming from the state-owned Bharat Sanchar Nigam Limited (BSNL). That signal was transmitted from the island of Sandeshkhali, about 20 kilometers away. There is electricity in Sandeshkhali, but it is a very intermittent supply. BSNL used batteries to store the power and beam the signal. The batteries had failed, the company told us and would need to be replaced from Calcutta—a process that would take months.

The School in the Cloud at Korakati became desolate and empty. Children would walk miles daily to check whether the internet was back, waiting for hours outside when they discovered it was not or playing the same mindless game on the computers. Then they would walk away. About three months later, Ashis and his engineer, Ranabir, found a private service provider that promised a strong and reliable signal. The internet returned to Korakati, better than ever before. The children reappeared.

RESULTS

Over the next two years (2014–2016), Ritu Dangwal spent several days every month in the guest room at Korakati. It was a magical experience for her, about as different from living in Delhi as it can be. During this time, she worked with a sample group of children—measuring reading comprehension with the ASER tests, self-confidence levels using the instrument created by Suneeta, and internet searching skills using my developing assessment tool (see Figure 2.4 and Figure 2.5). Three graphs, Figure 4.3, Figure 4.4, and Figure 4.5, reveal the magic that began to occur in Korakati.

When the Korakati SinC first opened, the starting reading comprehension scores were 20 percent, on average, which means the children could barely mumble a text out loud, let alone understand any of it. In the first three months of the program, Ritu reported to us that the scores had climbed steeply upward to nearly 60 percent. She was in awe. A self-organizing system was producing spontaneous order before her very eyes.

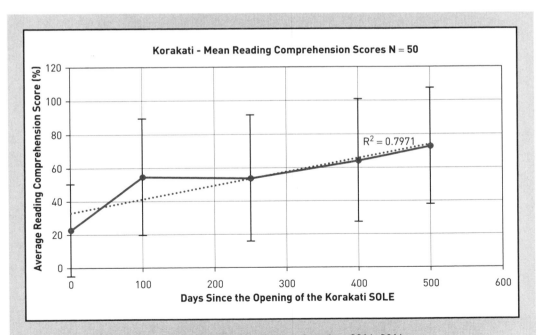

Figure 4.3 Korakati: Improvement in Reading Comprehension, 2014–2016

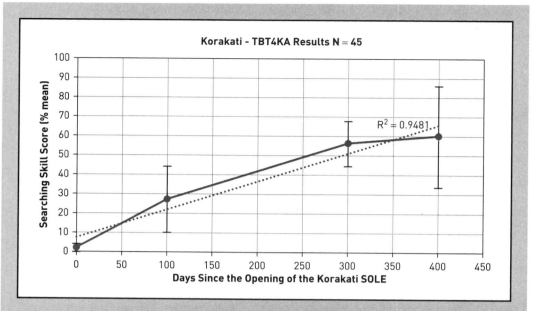

Figure 4.4 Korakati: Improvement in Searching Skills, 2014–2016

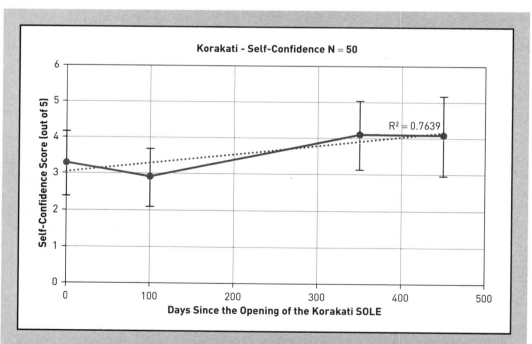

Figure 4.5 Korakati: Measurements of Children's Self-Confidence Levels

The flat line on the graph in Figure 4.3 between days 120 and 220 illustrates the effect that the internet outage had on the development of reading comprehension. The correlation between the absence of the internet and the stagnation of growth in reading comprehension matched almost perfectly. It was as if a strange and alien teacher had been absent.

During 2015, reading comprehension scores in Korakati increased to an average that was close to 80 percent. The children of Korakati were reading just about as well as the children in Gateshead, England! Their accents were a mixture of Bengali, good Granny English, and a bit of Geordie (inhabitants of Newcastle). I loved every word.

Using my TBT4KA test for internet searching skills (see Figure 2.4), Ritu also measured the children's ability to search on the internet. The data showed an unambiguous upward line (Figure 4.4).

The children at Korakati had gone from an average searching ability of 0 percent to 60 percent in a little over a year. Now you might wonder why you can't see the same flat line between days 120 and 220 when the internet was absent. Actually, it was a simple problem with measurement. The TBT4KA is a harder test to administer than the reading comprehension test. Moreover, it cannot be administered when the internet is not available. It was quite hard for Ritu to get her sample group together and test them each time she was in Korakati. During the entire period, she was able to measure only four times, hence the four data points on the graph.

So, what effect did SinC have on the self-confidence of the children in the remote Sundarbans? Ritu's measurements of the self-confidence of the children, using the test devised by Suneeta, produced a strange graph (Figure 4.5).

On a 5-point scale, the children had started out at about 3.3 and reached 4.0 in a little over a year. An insignificant change.

When we started the experiment, it was not as though the children were reticent or nervous or scared—they were eager and poised to jump in and use the computers. In all my years of experiments since the Hole-in-the-Wall project of 1999, I have never seen children looking nervous or insecure about computers and the internet. It was no different in Korakati. It was as if the children and the internet were waiting for each other.

I used to think that children's self-confidence would increase as they got better at using the internet. Our self-confidence assessment results in Korakati were the first indication that this hypothesis is flawed.

I can't really explain the digital self-confidence in the children of this generation. I still see elderly people afraid to touch a computer because they might press a wrong key and it might "blow up." Maybe we have moved from that world to one where things

> "
> *I have never seen children looking nervous or insecure about computers and the internet. It was as if the children and the internet were waiting for each other.*

don't blow up and our children, everywhere, know that. What a story of hope that would be!

The story of the School in the Cloud in Korakati would not be complete without the story of Milan Mondal.

During the period of the experiment, the people who supervised the School in the Cloud at Korakati changed. When the project began in March 2014, the facility supervisor was a local teacher, Aurobindo, who left within months when he realized he was not required to teach. His replacement was a young man from Calcutta, Aniket, who survived for almost a year before succumbing to the infections and insects of the Sundarbans. He went back to Calcutta. During all this time, the various supervisors were assisted by another young man, a boy really, called Milan, and by a girl, Hemlata, who was in charge of cleaning the facility. After Aniket left in 2015, Ashis put Milan in charge.

From 2015 until the writing of this chapter (July 2018), the School in the Cloud at Korakati has become the best of all the sites we built. It is spotlessly clean, well appointed, with working computers, electricity, and the internet. Attendance is high, and the Granny Cloud interacts regularly with the children. Mothers bring their children from miles away. The parents say they have never before seen a school like this one—the children ask to go. Milan has become a supremely confident, minimally invasive teacher. He knows no other way. His English has improved immensely, and he blogs and posts on Facebook regularly. His life is transformed.

Unfortunately, the parents in Korakati have no means to pay for the upkeep of the facility. The money I got from the TED Prize is finished. I got a bit more from the Dalio Foundation in the United States, for which I am extremely grateful. But by the fall of 2018, there will be no more funds to keep Korakati operational. I would very much like to find an economic model for people who just can't pay. Short of a miracle, Korakati will close down and become an abandoned building or a cowshed. Critics from all around the world will then visit and publish papers on how the School in the Cloud did not work, just as they did for the Hole-in-the-Wall sites after funding for them had run out.

AREA 2: CHANDRAKONA, WEST MIDNAPORE, BENGAL, INDIA

The history of Midnapore is one of chaos, politics, and plunder. For the region, the seventh century was a prosperous but lawless period, described by a curious Sanskrit word—*matsyanyaya*—that means "the justice system of the fish." This word encapsulates the idea that big fish eat little fish, or the strong consume the weak, in periods of chaos.

In the fifteenth century, one of the kings of the region, Chandraketu, modestly named the biggest city Chandrakona after himself. He was a biggish fish. Then the

Islamic rulers (even bigger fish) overpowered the last of the Hindu kingdoms. By then, Chandrakona had a thriving weaving industry producing exquisite silk and other textiles. Then a seriously big fish entered the pond.

Chandrakona came under the British East India Company in 1760. While the British brought in law and order of sorts, they also took a look at what the weavers of Chandrakona were producing. It took them very little time to realize that they could use their new political powers to eliminate competitors and exploit the weavers of Chandrakona. A little more law-and-order later and we see cotton manufactured in Manchester and Birmingham replacing Indian cottons on world markets. The weavers of Chandrakona either relocated or became potato farmers. The looms of Chandrakona stopped. Over the centuries, the people of Midnapore learned to survive by cunning, lying, stealing, and misguiding their foreign rulers in every way possible. They hate injustice.

After I was awarded the TED Prize in 2013, Bimal Basu contacted me to ask if I would set up a School in the Cloud in Chandrakona. It was the first time I had heard of the place.

Ashis went to Chandrakona in March of 2013. Mr. Basu's organization is called Sarbik Palli Kalyan Kendra. It is located in a village called Kiageria, a few miles from Chandrakona city. It's a rustic place, with mud-walled cottages, mud paths, and the

Figure 5.1 The Chandrakona Site Before the School in the Cloud Was Built

smell of earth, hay, and cows. Kiageria is surrounded by miles of potato plantations in every direction. A great number of India's potatoes come from this part of the country. In fact, when you are presented with a plate of French fries (or "chips" in England), anywhere in the world, you might very well be tasting a bit of Kiageria.

Ashis instantly liked the place. It was not as difficult to get to as Korakati, and it had electricity. To get to Kiageria, one can take excellent highways out of Calcutta for most of the way. The journey takes about three hours. We did not know the name Kiageria when we started off—we, including Mr. Basu, called it Chandrakona. In what follows, I will use Kiageria and Chandrakona interchangeably.

I was honored to be at the School in the Cloud at Chandrakona when it was inaugurated on March 13, 2014, four days after the inauguration of the Korakati site. I think it is one of the best-looking SinC locations we built. There is a large hall for the computers and the Skype screen, toilets for the children, and two guest rooms with attached bathrooms and a tiny lobby for guests. A local ISP provides reasonably good bandwidth for the internet. Next to the School in the Cloud is a small temple. The idols that once graced the temple had been stolen years ago, and the place was decrepit. We repaired the structure and put in new idols, Krishna and Radha. A local Brahmin keeps the temple going. The internet keeps the rest going.

Figure 5.2 The School in the Cloud at Kiageria, Chandrakona

Video 5.1:
Chandrakona

Videos may also
be accessed at
**resources
.corwin.com/
schoolinthecloud**.

You can view the children of Chandrakona in a short video excerpt from *The School in the Cloud* film—see Video 5.1.

A group of local adolescents often hung around the campus playing carom (also known as finger billiards, this game is played on a wooden board). They were most enthusiastic about the School in the Cloud until I explained to them it was for children under the age of 15. In each of our Schools in the Cloud, we had an age cap of 15. This was to keep the adolescents from taking over the facility, particularly in the more remote areas. However, in Chandrakona, Mr. Basu hired one of them to be the supervisor and another, older man, to take care of cleanliness and maintenance. To protect their identity, I will refer to them as Amabasya and Kalidas. Ashis paid them from the project funds.

LEARNING AND SOME CHALLENGES

After the facility opened, children started flocking to the Chandrakona School in the Cloud, but the internet connection from a local ISP turned out to be shaky, and after a few weeks, the children reported that the computers were very slow.

Ashis sent his engineer, Ranabir, to investigate. Ranabir had built the computers and set up the network and internet. Upon investigation, Ranabir found that what he had put into the computers (e.g., hard disks, RAMs) had been replaced by equipment of lesser value. The hard disks were of smaller capacity than the originals; similarly, the RAMs (random access memories) were smaller than what he had put in. It turns out that a small business had started in the village, upgrading the hard disks and RAMs of people who owned computers in the city to a higher capacity for a very low cost. As a result, the computers in the School in the Cloud had become nearly unusable.

Amabasya and Kalidas denied knowing anything about this. In fact, they could not believe it had happened. Mr. Basu was shocked, and Ashis asked if he should call in the police. In the end, the computers were repaired, and the backs of the units, where the disks and the RAMs could be accessed, were sealed off with duct tape. Ashis removed Amabasya as the supervisor and brought in a new supervisor, Joydeb.

Ranabir then installed a web camera in the room and configured it so that its broadcast could be seen on a smart phone. The School in the Cloud in Chandrakona became operational again. Ritu collected a random sample of 64 children and began her measurements.

Joydeb kept the facility going against severe resistance from Kalidas and Amabasya. But then a different problem arose. Girls stopped coming.

The local parents knew Amabasya and were willing to let their daughters come to the School in the Cloud when he was the supervisor. But they did not know Joydeb and were reluctant to let their daughters come to a facility managed by a male stranger. I suggested that a second supervisor, a woman, be hired. Sumita Mondol seemed the perfect fit. The girls returned.

One of the girls, Piya, regularly attended from 2014 to 2018. In Jerry Rothwell's documentary, *The School in the Cloud* (2018), which spans three years, Piya grows up into a young woman with a fixed ambition. She wants to join the police force. The internet played a significant role in the development of her aspiration. Through the School in the Cloud, she researched the role and benefits of women in police forces and, much against the wishes of her parents, resolved to be become a police officer.

Other children were using YouTube to learn all sorts of things. On one of my visits, they showed me a toy vehicle they had built using a plastic bottle, a small fan to propel it, and wheels made of cardboard. Joydeb, who understood minimally invasive education quite well by then, provided encouragement, as did the Granny Cloud.

In June of 2014, Kalidas insisted that someone should sleep in the room for added security. A few months later, Ashis and Ranabir began to notice some odd changes. In the mornings, the computers would be found facing the rear wall of the room, placed such that their screens could not be seen. The web camera would often be found turned toward a wall instead of toward the room. One night, Ashis looked at the camera image from his residence in Calcutta and saw a group of adolescent boys along with Amabasya (the fired manager) viewing pornographic sites. They had forgotten to turn the web camera away that night.

Ashis went off to Chandrakona and reported the matter to Mr. Basu, who summoned the boys. All of them vehemently denied any knowledge of the matter and suggested that the children who came to the facility during the day were the culprits. Those children were 6 to about 13 years old and used the computers in heterogeneous groups of boys and girls. The camera images said otherwise, but we did not press the matter, hoping that our warning would be a sufficient deterrent.

In July 2017, Joydeb left. He had become quiet and distraught; I suspect that he was being bullied by the adolescents into letting them in at night. The School in the Cloud in Chandrakona began to falter. Kalidas began to ask for more money for anything he could think of.

In addition, something was happening to Sumita. She was increasingly on a neurotic and religious "trip" of some sort. As she explained it, a "God woman" from somewhere appeared and was living with her. Then, one day, a little boy dropped the mouse while working on one of the computers. Something snapped in Sumita Mondol. "Who will pay for the repairs, your father?" she said to the terrified child. Then she punished him severely, using physical force. I asked Ashis to remove Sumita immediately and not to let her come near the facility. Later, she was frequently seen in the village talking with Kalidas.

After all of this, Ashis recommended closing down the site and redistributing the money to the other Schools in the Cloud. In 2017, funding for the School in the Cloud at Chandrakona was stopped.

However, during these turbulent years, Ritu had continued with her data collection and had become friends with everyone in the village. Ritu is a striking-looking woman—the adolescent troublemakers were no match for her. The data from the tests on reading comprehension, internet searching ability, and self-confidence were fascinating (see Figures 5.3, 5.4, and 5.5).

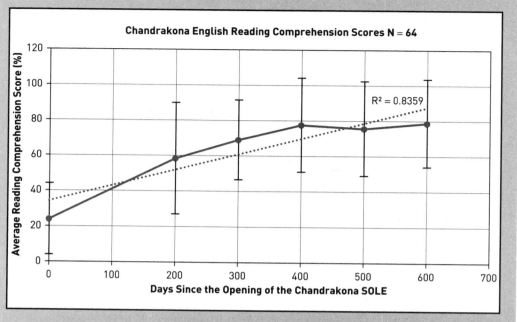

Figure 5.3 Chandrakona: Improvement in Reading Comprehension, 2014–2017

Within one year, reading comprehension scores had risen from less than 40 percent to well over 80 percent. The dip in the graph between days 400 and 500 probably reflects the effects of the thefts and misconduct that took place in the school.

During the "stable" period from Day 200 to 400, we can see a rapid rise in searching skills, from close to zero to over 50 percent (Figure 5.4). When things are not so fine, for example, in the first six months when the computers and internet connections were being sorted and then in the days after Day 400 when the mischief began, the progress is flat.

I have seen this time and again in our experiments—computers and the internet must work flawlessly for the spontaneous order of minimally invasive education to thrive.

The self-confidence test scores in Chandrakona, through its troubled history, tell an unexpected story.

As shown in Figure 5.5, the self-confidence graph is flat, unperturbed. The children in Chandrakona are supremely confident of their abilities with computers, and possibly they feel they can cope with whatever life offers. Perhaps their 1,500-year history of chaotic misrule has steeled their very genes to take things as they come.

About six months after the Chandrakona School in the Cloud was closed down in 2017, Mr. Basu attempted to reopen it. After Mr. Basu, one of the young men wrote to me that he could get the facility up and running again. I gave him some money, but as of this writing, I am not aware of whether or not this endeavor was successful.

The land of *matsyanyaya* awaits the next big fish.

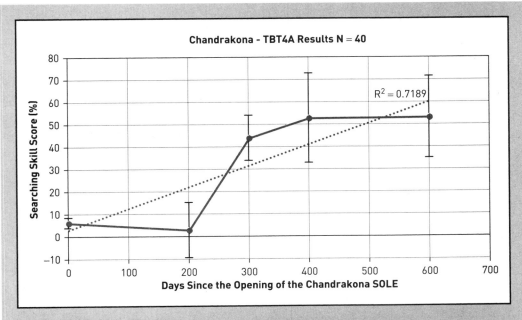

Figure 5.4 Chandrakona: Improvement in Searching Skills, 2014–2017

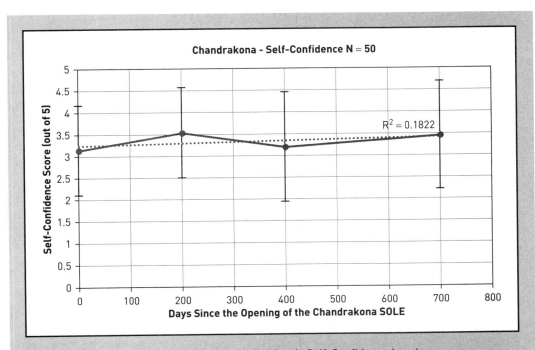

Figure 5.5 Chandrakona: Measurements of Children's Self-Confidence Levels

AREA 3: KALKAJI, NEW DELHI, INDIA

Kalkaji is in the south of New Delhi. It is here that, in the mid-1990s, NIIT (an Indian multinational company that offers learning management and training delivery solutions to corporations, institutions, and individuals) located its headquarters.

From 1962 to 2006, I lived, studied, and worked in Delhi except for the four years when I went to Calcutta to study. I understand Delhi and its history well. Delhi is one of the oldest continuously inhabited cities in the world. Empire after empire made Delhi its capital, and each new ruler built on top of the deposed empires' structures. Delhi's history is steeped in intrigue, politics, transitory power, and lies. It is a city where who you know is far more important than what you know. To me, it is one of those places that you never miss when you finally leave, no matter how long you have lived there.

Begun in 1999, the original Hole-in-the-Wall site was closed down in 2006 because the Government of Delhi wanted to build a parking lot. The children were disgusted, and NIIT was a bit annoyed, although the company never said so. Instead, NIIT built two Hole-in-the-Wall computers on the boundary wall of a nearby government school called the "Government Girls/Boys Senior Secondary School No. 3" (GGSSS/GBSSS). To the slum children, the site was neither safe nor publicly visible. A few came, but furtively.

THE EARLY SOLE AT GGSSS/GBSSS

This government school in Kalkaji is actually two schools in one. In the morning it's a girl's school and in the afternoon, after the girls have left, it becomes a boys school, with different staff. An ingenious way to use the same space twice!

In 2010, I met Richard Alberg, CEO and founder of MWS Technology, a vocational education and employment company. After hearing me speak at an event, Richard was impressed by the idea of self-organized learning and, later, offered to donate £5000 for any of my projects.

When the money arrived a few months later, I wrote to Ritu asking if we could set up a room for SOLEs in GGSSS. The principal, Geetha Devi, grasped the concept quickly and, indeed, was aware of the earlier Hole-in-the-Wall experiments. She was eager to set up a room for SOLEs. She showed me a tiny room next to the library where this could happen.

I wrote to Mrs. Devi from England asking if we could start in October 2010, and requesting that she obtain the necessary permissions from the government. Geetha Devi asked Ritu to go ahead immediately. It was only much later that she explained to me that she had not obtained any permission from the Education Department of Delhi. If she had, she assured me, the project would have been delayed forever.

Vikram Kumar, who used to work with me back in the NIIT days, built the SOLE room in GGSSS. We let the girls in on February 8, 2011. Ten days later, I wrote to Richard to report to him on the immediate impact of his funds.

LEARNING

February 18, 2011

Dear Richard:

The SOLE constructed with your donation became operational on February 8, 2011. I started it off with a group of 17 children and a question, "Are there robots that can clean rooms by themselves?"

The principal of the school said the children's English was very poor and they needed instruction on how to use computers.

I left the children to do what they could. No teachers, no instruction.

Thirty minutes later, a little girl said, "The Roomba can do the job; it will be available in India shortly." Another said, "It doesn't really matter what a robot does; its basic engineering is mostly the same." These were 11-year-olds.

The principal said, tearfully, "I have underestimated my children all these years, I will change everything from tomorrow."

Thank you, Richard, for this opportunity.
Sugata Mitra

I had chosen the question about room-cleaning robots because many of the girls in GGSSS were daughters of housecleaners who worked in the richer neighborhoods of Delhi. I thought the girls would say that their mothers would lose their jobs because of robots. They did not.

The little girls of Kalkaji said, "When the robots arrive, our mothers will not have to be housecleaners anymore." I felt small and ashamed.

By the time I got the TED Prize in 2013, the girls in GGSSS were familiar with SOLEs and extremely fond of their "lab." Their English had progressed beyond all expectations.

After the TED Prize, I decided to update the GGSSS facility into an official School in the Cloud. I gave Ritu a small fund, much smaller than the amounts we had spent on Korakati, Chandrakona, and Gocharan, and, with the help of Vikram, Ritu refurbished the facility within a few months.

Figure 6.1 The School in the Cloud at the Government Girls Senior Secondary School (GGSSS), Kalkaji, New Delhi

Video 6.1:
Under Secretary
of State for Public
Diplomacy and
Public Affairs Rick
Stengel Visits
India

Videos may also
be accessed at
**resources
.corwin.com/
schoolinthecloud**.

The School in the Cloud at GGSSS, Kalkaji, was inaugurated on February 4, 2014. Ritu started with a new set of children who were too young to have used the earlier SOLE room. She began her usual testing.

In November 2014, Richard Stengel visited the School in the Cloud at Kalkaji and spoke to the girls. The YouTube video *Under Secretary of State for Public Diplomacy and Public Affairs Rick Stengel Visits India* summarizes his visit (see Video 6.1). The video is one of the best endorsements of the School in the Cloud. The Kalkaji girls had left him emotionally spellbound.

During those three years of testing, the girls changed immensely. I visited the site several times, and each time was an astonishing revelation. Two incidents particularly come to mind.

Deepa, a 12-year-old girl, had put up a striking picture of the Andromeda galaxy as the desktop background for one of the computers. I asked if she was interested in stars and the universe. She nodded.

"So, are you going to become an astronomer when you grow up?" I asked.

"Mmm," said Deepa, hesitatingly.

"Maybe you want to become a space scientist?"

"No," said Deepa.

I was a bit puzzled by her replies. The other girls around were listening intently.

"You like that picture on the desktop, don't you?" I probed.

Deepa had a strange, anguished expression on her face. This was getting very strange. Suddenly, she burst out, clearly and loudly.

"I want to know *why* it's there," said Deepa.

Something went tingling down from my head toward my feet. Here was a girl asking about the reason for the existence of the universe!

"No one knows why it's there," I whispered. Ritu said it was time for us to go.

On another occasion, Ritu showed me the video of another girl, Jaya. She too was 12. A year in the School in the Cloud had made her not just a fluent speaker but a girl with an attitude. Jaya wanted to become a lawyer. In the video, she says that poor people are sometimes punished just because they are poor. She wants to change that. She would challenge why the wrong people are punished by the law.

William Sloan and Daniel Oxenhandler, two young filmmakers, worked for several years to make a film about the Kalkaji girls. Their documentary, *The Open Window*, premiered in April 2019 in Copenhagen just as this book is going into production (Birkegaard, Oxenhandler, & Sloan, 2018).

The School in the Cloud in Kalkaji was doing fabulously well. There were just a few challenges here, mostly to do with scheduling because the room was too small. Principal Geetha Devi made it all work. She is a remarkable example of the importance of school leadership.

But fascinating, qualitative anecdotes don't tell the whole story. Ritu's quantitative data tells the other half of that story of change and growth.

RESULTS

Figure 6.2 shows that by the end of the study, the girls at Kalkaji had reading comprehension scores close to 90 percent of what they should be at that age—anywhere in the world. However, you will notice that we started with a high baseline score of around 60 percent. SOLEs and Granny sessions had been in the school two years before our measurements started, thanks to Richard Alberg. Would the results have been the same if there had been no School in the Cloud? Geetha Devi did not think so, based on past scores at the same school. But then, the same tests had not been administered in the past. Sometimes you know that an intervention has worked, but you can't really prove it. I only know that the girls at Kalkaji can read and understand what they were reading better than people of their age at most places on the planet—and I had been to many.

Within the first year of the SinC's operation, the average score for internet searching skills had gone up from near zero to over 80 percent (see Figure 6.3). Would this have happened if the School in the Cloud had not been there? Since the regular school curriculum had nothing about searching on the internet, there is good reason to believe that the improvement was solely due to the work done in the SinC. Ritu could not continue this measurement beyond the first year (2014) because of operational difficulties. The school was beginning to change. More about that change in a moment.

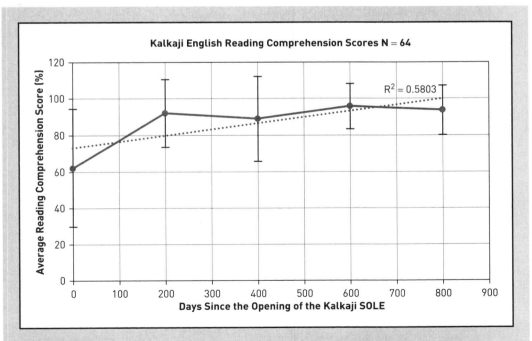

Figure 6.2 Kalkaji: Improvement in Reading Comprehension, 2014–2017

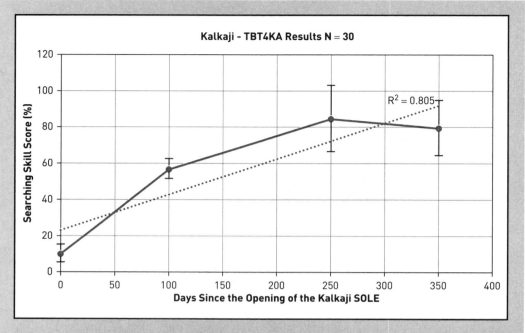

Figure 6.3 Kalkaji: Improvement in Searching Skills, 2014–2015

Figure 6.4 shows the self-confidence test scores over one and a half years. You will notice a small but clearly visible drop between Day 100 and 400. It is not significant, I think. The girls were supremely confident to start with, and they remained so!

Geetha Devi retired as the principal in 2015, about a year and a half after the School in the Cloud was set up in Kalkaji.

Geetha Devi was replaced. Ritu said the new lady principal was hard as nails; I did not believe her. In the only meeting I had with the new principal, she was most polite and cordial. However, I had a misgiving I could not really identify. Finally, I asked her.

"Is there something about the School in the Cloud that is bothering you, Madam?"

As though a dam had burst, the principal's voice lashed out at me.

"The girls! They have become ill mannered, overconfident, and belligerent. They confront their teachers and point out errors, not just in what they are teaching but in their pronunciation!"

"They have lost sight of their position in society; they think they can become anything."

As I listened to her speak, I believed what she was really trying to convey was something such as the following: "If this is allowed to go on, where will we get our maid servants from?"

I went back, one last time, to the School in the Cloud at GGSSS. I tried to explain to the girls to tone it down, to play dumb. They looked at me, their long-time friend, with wide uncomprehending eyes.

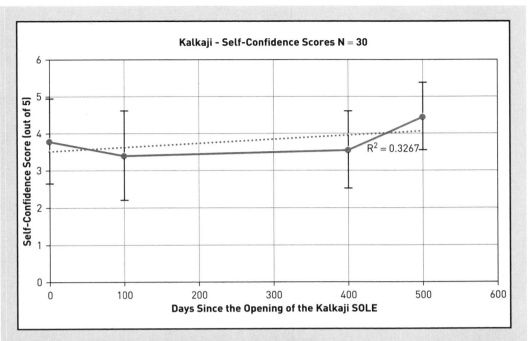

Figure 6.4 Kalkaji: Measurements of Children's Self-Confidence Levels

A few months into 2016, I received a devastating email from Ritu.

> ... there seems to be a not so good situation in Kalkaji. The entire school is moving to a new building in the same premise. Just learnt that they are demolishing the SOLE lab and the Principal's Office. There is no free room for the SOLE lab. Spoke with principal & for the time being, we are keeping the equipment in the science lab. I might have to take the equipment with me, if principal insists.
>
> So, for the time being, the lab will be closed.
>
> I am very worried. . . .
>
> Ritu Dangwal, PhD
> Research & Project Coordinator
> TED Prize 2013 project
> The School in the Cloud

The School in the Cloud at Kalkaji was closed in June 2016. It never reopened.

AREA 4: PHALTAN, DISTRICT SATARA, MAHARASHTRA, INDIA

The first four Schools in the Cloud had a socioeconomic and geographical spread from the impoverished and undeveloped Sundarbans to the rural poor of Chandrakona and from the urban lower middle class of Gocharan in the east to the urban slums of Delhi in the north of India. We now needed a location that was both urban and middle class. Suneeta chose a location in the far west of India, a school in a town called Phaltan.

Phaltan is old. Its ruling family during the days of the British Empire, the Nimbalkars, could trace its ascendency back to the reign of the Bahmani sultans of the 1300s. It is interesting that a local family with a similar name came to play such an important part in our story and in the modern history of the region—the Nimbkar family.

In the 1930s, American Elizabeth Lundy married engineer Vishnu Nimbkar and took the name Kamala Nimbkar; she became a pioneer in the field of occupational therapy in India. A school for disadvantaged children was named in her honor. In 1978, another remarkable American, Maxine Berntsen, formed an organization for child development called Pragat Shikshan Sanstha (PSS) of which the Kamala Nimbkar Balbhavan (KNB) school formed a part. We call this school PSS–Phaltan, or PSSP for short. It is headed by Dr. Manjiri Nimbkar, granddaughter of Kamala Nimbkar and daughter of Bonbehari Nimbkar, a renowned and awarded agriculturist in India.

Suneeta decided to build a School in the Cloud at PSSP. Manjiri Nimbkar was a bit aware of my work and agreed enthusiastically.

The School in the Cloud at Phaltan was inaugurated on December 3, 2014.

PSSP is recognized by the government but not funded. The language of instruction is Marathi. The School in the Cloud is in a room in front of the school, clearly visible from the road outside. Suneeta had started Granny Cloud activities there in

Figure 7.1 The School in the Cloud at Phaltan

June 2013, using an old computer. Manjiri and most parents felt that the children were at a disadvantage because of their limited knowledge of English.

The facility we created is described in Suneeta's report:

> The SOLE Room is a rectangular-shaped area with a floor space of about 225 square feet [my estimate]. It is large enough to house five desktop computers with U-shaped tables and colorful chairs, plus one laptop connected to the screen TV. The lab has the trademark glass windows, but these are French windows, sized and sliding, so as to make the most of the breeze outside. Shutters have been installed, which are pulled down at night to ensure safety.
>
> The children took part in the design process, since they had already experienced Granny sessions for a few months. Internet facilities were quite good to begin with. In the past year, the demand for internet facilities has grown significantly across Phaltan, causing uncertain bandwidth availability at the lab. Because of the positioning of the camera, the view during Skype sessions for the grannies is restricted primarily to the children sitting directly in front of the webcam. The lab has an administrative coordinator and an administrative assistant, who are both available to support sessions mainly for the primary school children. Other teachers and staff are available during individual sessions for observations and have been trained to be unobtrusive. The cleaning and general maintenance is taken care of by the children themselves on a rotating basis, helped by the teachers.
>
> The school has a total of 450 children, from preschool to Grade 10. They come from very diverse socioeconomic backgrounds and have parents from all walks of life. However, the bulk of children come from poor socioeconomic backgrounds. Although 52 percent pay the relatively cheap fees, 29 percent of the children pay no fees at all, and another 19 percent pay half the fee. The medium of learning is Marathi, which is also the regional language. English is taught as one subject at the school. Twenty percent of the students come from the nearby rural areas, with some travelling as many as 15 kilometers to school each way.
>
> The SinC lab is used by Grades 1 to 7 for scheduled sessions either for free usage [when about 15–18 children, or half a class, come in at the same time] or with Grannies when groups of five to eight come in for more small-group interaction. Since June 2016, the school has also extended the use of the lab to the preschool section, so about 340 children in the school get a chance to go to the lab once a week.
>
> The lab operates six days a week [Monday to Saturday], typically from 8:00 a.m. to 5:30 p.m. Grades 1 to 3 usually use it in the morning shift [7:30 a.m. to 12:30 p.m.], while Grades 4 to 7 use the lab during the afternoon shift [12:30 pm to 5:30 pm].
>
> There are usually three Granny sessions scheduled every day.

Suneeta began her measurements at Phaltan with five groups of children—from Year 2, 3, 4, 5, and 6. She also measured Year 7, 8, and 9, but we did not use these data because these children were already accustomed to Granny sessions. Suneeta measured a total of 170 children across the year-based groups for about two years. It was the most extensive of the measurements we have done. I thought it was an impossibly ambitious data sequence to measure. I was wrong.

Suneeta measured reading comprehension carefully, using the ASER and other tests described previously. She also measured children's aspirations. I have not included the aspirations data because I do not think they contribute to our understanding of what the School in the Cloud does for children. There are many influences on the development of children's aspirations including parents, teachers, and other role models. We do not have enough evidence if the School in the Cloud can change those aspirations, although you will see anecdotal evidence that it does, sometimes. There is more work to be done.

Suneeta did not measure self-confidence or internet searching skills in Phaltan. Her reasons were interesting. She said the children's self-confidence scores went up faster than our measurement schedule! In a matter of hours, the scores would touch 3 on a scale of 5. Children born in a digital age are confident about operating devices and figuring things out. They may be shy and nervous in examinations where they have to prove what they "know" without any assistance from devices, but they are not shy or reticent when they have access to the internet.

Suneeta did not measure internet searching skills in Phaltan either because she felt that the test I had devised needed to be validated and standardized. This time I did not agree with her for the reasons I laid out in Chapter 2.

During the years that the Phaltan SinC was in operation (2014–2017), children progressed approximately two grade levels (Year 2 went to Year 4, Year 4 to Year 6, and so on). Suneeta's data on reading comprehension speaks to us of those years of diligent, difficult, and meticulous measurements.

But the data is not what a student of natural science would call "clean." Suneeta collected many measurements, when she could and the best she could. Children in a school are not like subatomic particles in a particle accelerator: you can't measure what you want when you want. It is important to understand the data we collected at Phaltan so that you can appreciate the analyses. In what follows, I will describe the data Suneeta collected.

MAKING SENSE OF THE DATA FROM PHALTAN

The School in the Cloud at Phaltan provided us with a great deal of insight into the effects of SOLEs and Granny Cloud sessions on children of various ages. Suneeta went on data collection trips to Phaltan in November and December of 2014; in March, July, and September of 2015; and then in January, April, and August of 2016. That is a total of eight trips. During these trips, she sometimes stayed on, when she could, and took more than one set of measurements. In all, she took 13 sets of measurements. Not every set of measurements could cover all the children she wanted to measure, due to operational difficulties, holidays, football games, and things like that.

On her first visit, she chose her samples to be 36 children in Grade 2, 34 in Grade 3, 31 in Grade 4, 32 in Grade 5, and 37 in Grade 6. Her first visit was in November 2014, but the school year begins in August. So when she took her first set of measurements, all the grades were already three months or so into their school year. When she took her last set of measurements in August 2016, the original Grade 2 class had moved on to Grade 4, she called this sample G234, her cryptic message a simple reminder that children grow up!

When we apply this nomenclature to all the grades she started with we get these indicators: G234, G345, G456, G567, and G678. These are the five groups that Suneeta measured between November 2014 and August 2016. Table 7.1 helps show which groups were measured when.

Table 7.1 Measurements Taken at PSS–Phaltan, November 2014 to August 2016

School Year Start August 2014												Year 1 End July 2015				Year 2 End July 2016	
School Days	0	50	100	150	200	250	300	350	400	450	500	550	600	650	700	750	800
Measurement Days			0	50	100	150	200	250	300	350	400	450	500	550	600	650	700
Student Group																	
G234			x				x			x		x		x			x
G345			x		x			x		x					x		
G456			x	x				x		x							
G567			x					x					x		x		
G678			x		x			x									

Using these measurements, we can plot the progress of each group over the two years of measurements. But can we compare one group with another? I think there is a way we can. Suppose we want to compare the reading comprehension scores of G345 with those of G456 on Day 50 of the measurements (which is Day 150 of the school year). We have the measurements from G456 for that day but not from G345. We can approximate this missing data by looking at the data for G345 on Day 0 and Day 100 of our measurements (Day 100 and Day 200 of the school year). The simplest estimate is to join the two known points and take the midpoint. It is not the very best way to compare, but it is a reasonable guess, I think.

Using approximations such as this, we can compare different year groups. In what follows, you will see the story of SOLEs and reading comprehension in children. It's a story of hope.

WHAT THE PHALTAN DATA SAID

In Phaltan, Suneeta measured five groups of students over the course of 2014 to 2016. The first group, consisting of 36 children, was measured in Grade 2, Grade 3, and Grade 4. We'll call this group the Year 2 group. Their reading comprehension growth, plotted in Figure 7.2, follows an S-shaped pattern, showing improvement in reading comprehension from 0 percent to 27 percent.

To reiterate, the 36 children that Suneeta first measured at Grade 2 went from a reading comprehension score of zero to one of about 30 percent. It could have been because of what their teachers did during that time, or the increase could have been assisted by the School in the Cloud. We don't know.

The second group, consisting of 34 children, was measured in Grade 3, Grade 4, and Grade 5. We'll call this the Year 3 group. Their reading comprehension growth (Figure 7.3) shows as a nearly straight line of progress from 40 percent to 83 percent.

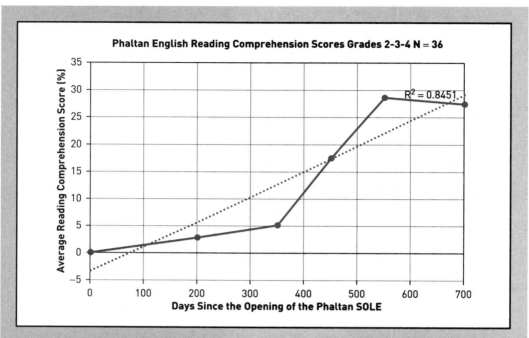

Figure 7.2 Phaltan: Reading Comprehension Improvement of Year 2 Group (Grades 2, 3, 4), 2014–2016

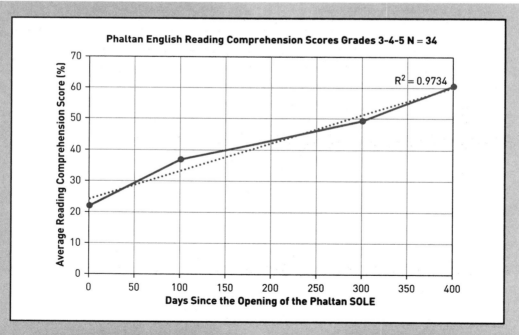

Figure 7.3 Phaltan: Reading Comprehension Improvement of Year 3 Group (Grades 3, 4, 5), 2014–2016

Notice that Figure 7.2 represents data collected by measuring a class of children beginning in Grade 2 and stretching over a three-year period, during which they went from Grade 2 to 3 to 4. Similarly, in Figure 7.3, we show results from a class of children who were first measured in Grade 3 and who progressed from Grade 3 to 4 to 5. The S-shaped plot of student learning in Figure 7.2 has changed to a nearly straight line in Figure 7.3. What happened? Remember, these are not the same children as those whose learning is shown in Figure 7.2. Figure 7.3 represents the learning of the next year's group.

The third group, consisting of 31 children, had their reading comprehension measured beginning in Grade 4 and continuing as they progressed through Grade 5 and 6. We'll call this the Year 4 group.

The students first measured in Grade 4 (Figure 7.4) reached close to 90 percent in reading comprehension proficiency over the two years of testing. They had started from a little over 42 percent. The straight-line growth appears again in Figure 7.4. Should the growth in reading comprehension scores be attributed to teachers or to the School in the Cloud?

The fourth group consisting of 32 children, had their reading comprehension measured beginning in Grade 5 and continuing as they progressed through Grade 6 and 7 (see Figure 7.5).

Reading comprehension scores for the students first measured in Grade 5 (the Year 5 group) shot up in a straight line from 50 percent to over 95 percent during

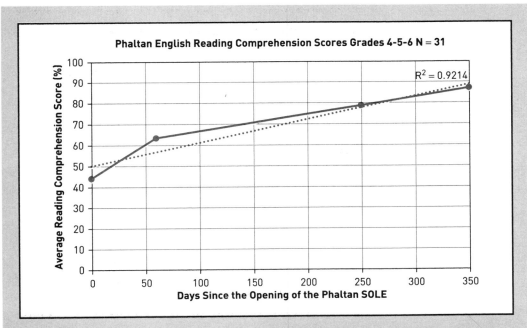

Figure 7.4 Phaltan: Reading Comprehension Improvement of Year 4 Group (Grades 4, 5, 6), 2014–2016

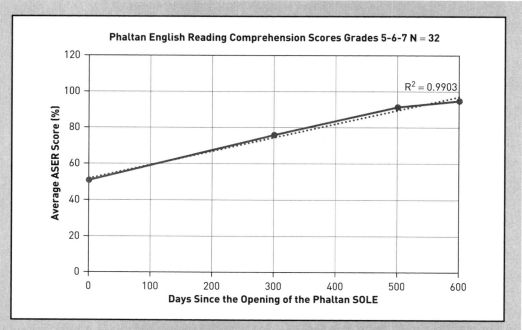

Figure 7.5 Phaltan: Reading Comprehension Improvement of Year 5 Group (Grades 5, 6, 7), 2014–2016

2014–2016 (see Figure 7.5). Is there some reason for this dramatic improvement that is attributable to more than "teaching and learning" approaches?

The fifth and last group, consisting of 37 children, had their reading comprehension measured beginning in Grade 6 and continuing as they progressed through Grade 7 and 8. We'll call this the Year 6 group.

In the measurements taken beginning in Grade 6, the linear trend continues (see Figure 7.6). Reading comprehension scores increased from 74 percent to nearly 96 percent.

These graphs are a fascinating hint of how growth in reading comprehension differs in different age groups. The youngest students' scores show a curious S-shaped plot whereas older students' scores show an upward curve and then steep straight lines, which start to flatten out for the oldest group of students. Is there a way to tell if these improvements in reading comprehension have anything to do with the School in the Cloud?

Suneeta measured the baseline reading comprehension scores for all five groups of students, those whose reading comprehension measurements were taken beginning in Grade 2, 3, 4, 5, and 6. These baselines tell us how well the children can read (in English) when they are taught by the usual methods in school—with no School in the Cloud inputs. Here is what she recorded:

If the baseline reading comprehension score for the Year 3 group is about 20 percent and that for the Year 4 group is about 45 percent, it should be reasonable to assume that, during Grade 3, reading comprehension scores would rise from

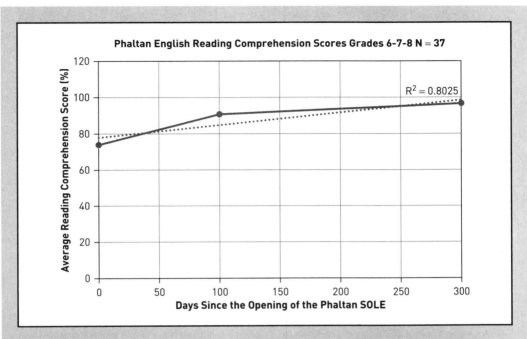

Figure 7.6 Phaltan: Reading Comprehension Improvement of Year 6 Group (Grades 6, 7, 8), 2014–2016

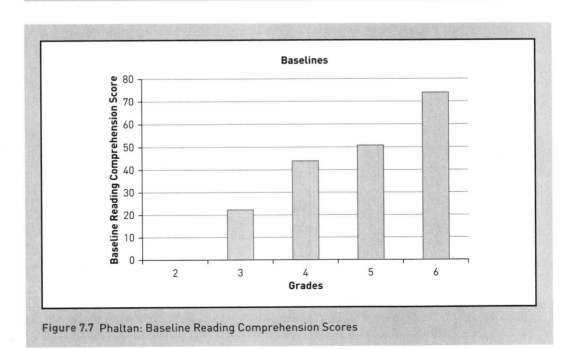

Figure 7.7 Phaltan: Baseline Reading Comprehension Scores

20 to 45 percent without the intervention of the School in the Cloud. In other words, we could expect traditional teachers, school curricula, and student development approaches to achieve at least this increase in reading comprehension.

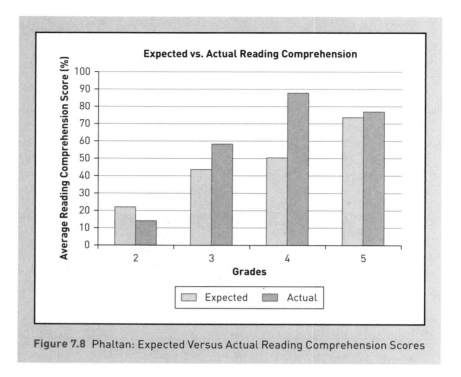

Figure 7.8 Phaltan: Expected Versus Actual Reading Comprehension Scores

Figure 7.8 shows that the actual reading comprehension scores, particularly for students in the Year 3 and Year 4 groups studied, indicate far more growth than expected. That's wonderful news! Clearly there is something influencing the unexpected growth. There was only one intervention in Phaltan during this time and that was the School in the Cloud.

Even better news! Phaltan continues to use the School in the Cloud vigorously. The principal and teachers support and understand the idea of self-organized learning. Here is a model that has worked.

There is a question that I have not yet been able to resolve, however. The School in the Cloud is a combination of two ideas—SOLEs and the Granny Cloud. Although the Phaltan data show us that the School in the Cloud does increase reading comprehension significantly, there is no way to tell the relative contributions of SOLE sessions and Granny sessions to this increase. For that, we would need a facility where the children do SOLE sessions but do not have access to any Granny sessions. I do not have these data yet. We can only conjecture that Granny sessions emphasize listening and speaking more than reading, while SOLE sessions are, almost exclusively, about reading. Maybe, it is SOLEs that contribute more to the increase in reading comprehension.

There is another anomaly in these incredible data from Suneeta. Why was the expected (or baseline) score to be achieved by the Year 2 group more than what was actually achieved by students using the School in the Cloud? Did we measure at the wrong time? What is going on with the S-shaped plot of the reading comprehension scores of very young children?

An intriguing answer may come from the village of Sidhuwal, 2000 kilometers to the north of Phaltan—in the fields of the Punjab.

But that is another story. One you will hear more about in Chapter 11.

AREA 5: KILLINGWORTH, NORTH TYNESIDE, ENGLAND

Killingworth is a town north of Newcastle upon Tyne in England. It is perhaps most famous for its nineteenth-century collieries. It is here that, in 1814, George Stephenson built his first steam engine, called the *Blücher*. The *Blücher* did not last very long, but it was the prototype from which George and his son Robert went on to build the famous *Rocket* steam engine at the Robert Stephenson and Company's Forth Street Works, close to today's Newcastle Central railway station.

From the quiet and, at the time, somewhat impoverished neighborhoods of Killingworth the literal engine of the Industrial Revolution began.

Amy-Leigh (then Dickinson) is a teacher and head of design technology and art at the George Stephenson High School (GSHS) in Killingworth. On April 18, 2012, Amy met Emma Crawley, a teacher and colleague of mine, and observed her in a SOLE session at St. Aidan's Primary School in Gateshead. Amy invited me to her school to see if her students, too, could use SOLEs. I used the opportunity to conduct an experiment on myself. I asked Amy not to tell me anything about the students I would be meeting—their ages, gender, what subjects they were doing—nothing. I also told her not to say anything to the students or their teacher about what I might be doing in their school.

As it turns out, I met with students in Year 7; they were about 12 years old. The topic was art. I met the art teacher and asked him what his plan would have been if I had not come. He said he was going to discuss the effect of light and shade on the still-life watercolors of Cézanne. I gulped. I had no clue what the teacher was talking about.

"Good morning," I said to the curious class. "Does anybody here have any idea what 'the effect of light and shade on the still-life watercolors of Cézanne' means?"

The children looked blankly at me and shook their heads. The teacher was sitting in the back of the classroom as I had requested him to do. Amy was hanging around, biting her nails.

"Well, we have to do something about this. Why don't you use the computers at the back and see if you can figure something out in 30 minutes?"

"Shall we work in groups?" asked a child.

"Just do what you want," I said.

Figure 8.1 The Killingworth Site Before the School in the Cloud

A SOLE followed. The art teacher came up to me and whispered, "Should we not help a bit? They don't even know how to spell Cézanne; they are typing Susan instead."

I shook my head. Google took the lead and figured out that if they were after still-life watercolors, they must mean Cézanne and not Susan.

Half an hour later, we heard the children describe the life of Cézanne, and how he started a new style with light and shade that is still followed today. They also discovered that his technique made still-life paintings look as though they were three-dimensional.

They had done all of what he would have done, the art teacher said, proudly. I had just "taught" an art class!

Amy continued with SOLEs in GSHS, and a few teachers started experimenting with it. They were encouraged by Ian Wilkinson, the principal. Ian had read of my work and found it interesting. Without his support, SOLEs in GSHS would never have succeeded. Newcastle University wrote to Amy asking her to send them a written description of her experience with SOLEs.

Amy's endorsement of SOLEs is one of the best I have ever received.

My name is Amy-Leigh Dickinson, and I am currently Curriculum Leader for Design and Art at George Stephenson High School. I have been asked to write a short letter on the impact Sugata Mitra and his work has had on me and on my school as a whole. I would first like to give some background to how I came across Sugata's work.

My head teacher, Ian Wilkinson, presented a whole-school assembly on Sugata Mitra and his work on the Hole in the Wall project. I was so interested in his work that I contacted the University of Newcastle and Sugata Mitra. I wanted to know if Sugata's work had been extended into teaching in secondary schools here in England. I was put in touch with Emma Crawley from St. Aidans School in Gateshead. I visited her school and watched a SOLE lesson in action. From there I was hooked!!! I was amazed by the results and was dying to get back to school to try it out. I was fortunate that Sugata came out to visit us at school and teach a Year 7 art class. [His] question was, "How can you paint a teardrop so it looks real?"

My first class was Year 8, and the question was, "Did you know rubies, diamonds, and emeralds are all made out of the same thing?" I explained to the class what a SOLE lesson was after showing them a clip of Sugata's TED talk. I will never forget this moment in my teaching career: I went from thinking "This will never work" to total amazement! The children learned so much from the lesson (as I myself did). This showed me that teaching could once more be exciting, unpredictable, and inspire children to think, take charge, be self-managers—and that most of them learn from each other, without me blocking and stopping the flow of lessons. I became so interested, I read Sugata Mitra's book Beyond the Hole in the Wall *and started to try it out with other classes (all different ages/stages). There were some fantastic results, and some not, but then that in itself proved interesting. I believe that by the time children are of the General Certificate of Secondary Education (GCSE) and A Level age (15–17), we have harmed their learning, as the curriculum/exam culture does not strive to create independent learners.*

I shared my research with Sugata and others, and within my school, SOLE became infectious; a number of teachers also started to try SOLE out. Due to my involvement with Sugata, I have been fortunate to meet a variety of wonderful dedicated people who are also supporters of Sugata and his work. This has had an impact on me and my own personal pedagogy.

Sugata's work fits perfectly into a number of our whole-school priorities, including collaboration and the development of independent thinkers. We are due to deliver [professional development] around SOLE after a further visit from Sugata when he spoke to the whole school and partner schools about his work. This provided a platform to showcase what SOLE is.

(Continued)

(Continued)

SOLE has had the following impact. . .

- *It has inspired me as a teacher and a lifelong learner to continue to investigate the future of learning for our students.*
- *The impact has been huge at George Stephenson High School. Whole-school continuing professional development (CPD) is being developed on SOLE and interwoven into our school priorities.*
- *I have been able to meet and network with likeminded teachers through SOLE to set up a network group to share practice across schools.*
- *I have started to develop SOLE planning groups with students; in these, they develop the follow-up lessons and indeed the big questions they have about the topics on offer.*
- *Some staff members have now tried SOLE out in their own classrooms, and data from these experiences are being collated.*
- *Sugata has proposed to continue to work with George Stephenson High School and develop a SOLE area within the school, a bookable resource usable by children at the school, by primary partner schools, and during the weekend. This will not only provide a SOLE platform but also rich data and experience that can be collated.*
- *I feel the biggest impact has been on the children that take part in SOLE lessons: the learning that is achieved is outstanding, and the levels of attainment are much higher than those seen in groups that are taught traditionally. I took two parallel groups in Year 8; one was the control group, the other the SOLE group. The measures were attainment, behaviour, and enjoyment. The SOLE group students were, in some cases, three levels higher than those in the control group.*
- *I have delivered a number of presentations on SOLE to groups of teachers, and this, in turn, has inspired others to try SOLE out. We regularly share our SOLE experiences through Twitter.*
- *After Sugata was awarded the TED Prize, I was fortunate enough to be contacted by TED to write about his work, and this led to hosting a Twitter conference. I now have contacts across the world who network when trying SOLEs out.*
- *I feel so privileged to have had the opportunity to work with Sugata and look forward to future projects. His work is so inspiring, and he has had a massive impact on me as a teacher and a person. It has given me the opportunity to meet teachers across the world, share practice, and bring this to my own school and staff.*

Amy-Leigh Dickinson
2013

Video 8.1:
George
Stephenson High
School

Videos may also
be accessed at
**resources
.corwin.com/
schoolinthecloud**.

The School in the Cloud at George Stephenson High School, Killingworth, was inaugurated on November 22, 2013. To hear Amy-Leigh Dickinson brainstorm ideas for the Killingworth School in the Cloud before it was built, watch Video 8.1 (Rothwell, 2018).

Amy followed my design exactly. The windows in the room were removed and replaced by larger windows. The furniture was mostly made of foam and reconfigurable to make different kinds of seating arrangements. The computers were at varying heights to enable younger children to see the screens easily. A false ceiling was put in and the electrical wiring came from the ceiling down though tubes. Each tube had a circular table attached to it where the computer was kept. There was a large screen on the wall for Skype. The walls of the room were writable surfaces.

Figure 8.2 Killingworth: The School in the Cloud

Amy wanted me to write something on a non-writable part of the wall—with a permanent marker! I was embarrassed, and the only line I could think of still adorns the wall:

"All mimsy were the borogoves. . . ."

Bit silly, but it was the best I could do.

I appointed a group of children "The Committee." They were charged with keeping an eye on how the facility was used. Amy and several other teachers began using the School in the Cloud (they called it the "SOLE room") regularly, under the watchful eyes of the Committee. A few weeks later, one of the Committee members said to me, "Mr. X was teaching in the SOLE room—should we talk to him or will you?" Concerned about what the children might say to him, I promised to talk to the teacher. Throughout the project, Amy kept peace.

On the day of the inauguration, we had two demonstrations for teachers and parents. The first was a SOLE conducted between a group of students located in a school in the United States and the Killingworth children. The topic was Hemingway's writing, and the session went brilliantly, with both groups working together with occasional, vociferous, disagreements.

The second demonstration was a SOLE with children who were about to start learning algebra.

I wrote a quadratic equation on the wall (an equation that I had copied from the internet before coming).

$$x^2 + 24x = 180$$

The children looked puzzled.

"Why are the letters and numbers all mixed up?"

"I don't know, what do you think?" I asked.

"I think its algebra," said one of the children.

"Well, can you figure out how much x is?" I asked.

"What do you mean how much is x? X is a letter!"

"Is it?" I asked.

The SOLE took off with very animated discussions. In the noisy hum of the SOLE, I began to hear the word "Damascus." I wondered what was going on. The hum began to soften, as it does in most SOLEs when major discoveries are made.

About 30 minutes later, I told the children we were running out of time; they needed to tell us what they had found.

What followed was an ancient story stretching from India to China, Babylon, Greece, and Persia. "Wars were fought over algebra," the children said with much satisfaction.

Clearly, they had been absorbed by the history of algebra. I had not thought of mathematics in this way. Is this, then, the way to create magic around what is often considered a dull and difficult subject?

However, time was running out, and I wanted to know if they had focused on my question.

"That is fantastic," I said. "But did you find out how much x is?"

"Six," said a little boy from the front row. "We found that out ages ago."

So they had found the solution, in minutes. Of course, they had not "solved" the equation—the internet had. But having found the answer, their focus had changed to the history of algebra. "What does this mean?" I asked the confused audience of teachers and parents.

The session ended. I thanked the children for a fantastic job, and they clapped. As I left the room, one of the children stepped up.

"By the way, Sugata, that equation has two answers," he said. "The other answer, if you know how to solve quadratic equations, or if you know how to Google, is −30 [minus thirty]."

I was stunned by the insight. My brain fogged as I left George Stephenson High School on that winter's day.

Whereas in India we tested for reading comprehension in English and English language fluency, we did not do so in England because the children were native English speakers. It would be interesting to know whether the School in the Cloud experience boosted growth in English students' reading comprehension scores over time or their ability to search online. Unfortunately, we did not have the assessment instruments necessary to measure that correlation. Instead, I tracked the usage of the SOLE room in GSHS. It increased steadily over time, and nearby primary schools started to use the facility as well. SOLEs are very much a part of school practice now in GSHS.

As the practice of SOLEs in a school becomes routine, there is the possibility that children, and possibly teachers, will begin to look at SOLEs as relaxed play-time. Children might spend a few minutes producing a presentation about the assigned question based on the first hits they get from the search engine. They then use the rest of the allotted SOLE time to play games. If this happens, I believe it is either because the question posed is not interesting enough to engage the children's attention, or because the question is not challenging enough or is too challenging. SOLEs are a delicate balance between order and chaos. They are easy to get wrong.

Second, if a group of children do too many SOLEs, say, one every day, then SOLEs become a routine they have to live with. It becomes "group work," or "inquiry." I have heard SOLEs described as such in England. It is a sure way to reduce SOLEs into a useless waste of time. For my thoughts on the recommended frequency of SOLE sessions, please see Chapter 10, the section titled "Creating and Posing Big Questions."

For now, the School in the Cloud at GSHS is in good use. In 2017, I received this email:

Hi Sugata,

You probably don't remember me, but I was a member of the SOLE committee at George Stephenson High School, and I was just wondering how the project is progressing. It still fills me with pride that I had the opportunity to be part of this project and how it has influenced my life choices. I just wanted to know if it is still growing to the extent that it was during my time with the project.

Sometimes, a few lines make life worth living. . . .

AREA 6: NEWTON AYCLIFFE, COUNTY DURHAM, ENGLAND

An hour's drive south of Killingworth (66 kilometers) is a town called Newton Aycliffe.

By 1825, Edward Pease's Stockton and Darlington Railway, of which George Stephenson was chief engineer, passed near Newton Aycliffe, where Stephenson's first steam railway locomotive, "Locomotion No. 1," was placed on the track. The area was marshy and covered in mist most of the time. During World War II, huge, grass-covered munitions factories were built here and serviced by the nearby railway line. Braving incredible dangers from the terrain and the Luftwaffe bombers, thousands of women worked here. They were called the "Aycliffe Angels."

In November of 2010, I came to know an Aycliffe Angel from our times. Her name is Katy Milne.

Katy is the director of arts and creativity at Greenfield Community College in Newton Aycliffe. She had read about my work and organized a workshop for teachers in the area on the use of SOLEs. Emma and I conducted the workshop.

Katy followed up with another meeting, to check what actions the teachers had taken. She followed up with a series of school visits and meetings. Paul Dolan, a teaching fellow at Durham University was invaluable in setting these up. Paul and I traveled all over County Durham, visiting schools and demonstrating SOLEs. The spread of SOLEs in North East England owes a lot to the work of Katy and Paul.

I spent a large part of 2011 and 2012 at the MIT Media Lab in the United States. During this time, Katy continued her work with SOLEs and often got me into meetings over Skype. The work that Katy and Paul did helped clarify the role of and justifications for SOLEs in school settings. Here is a sample report from Katy.

Figure 9.1 The Newton Aycliffe Site Before the School in the Cloud

May 15, 2012

Benefits of SOLEs:

- *Students have independently extended the resources beyond the computer to include books.*
- *The Project Manager and "Granny" roles have uncovered great qualities in students that are perhaps hidden in other contexts.*
- *Students have come up with amazing areas of interest to explore.*
- *Learning is taking place over a period of time.*

Challenges of SOLEs:

- *What question should we set next?*

  Ask the young people to help you with this. What do they think would be a good question?

- *How can we draw out the points in students' presentations to create new, stimulating, open, and engaging questions for subsequent sessions?*

  Try to find a different point from each group and draw something slightly different to add to the last group's point. Involve the students. Genuinely ask for their help in connecting the gathered information to new information and in identifying something that is genuinely interesting to explore. Can you perhaps apply the equality and gender investigation into the animal kingdom?

- *How will we prevent boredom with the general topic throughout the duration of this 10-week action research?*

  Try to set a question that remains open enough to be explored further. Encourage the students to help you find the next question.

- *How should we measure students' learning and depth of understanding of the topic?*

  There are two ways to look at this:

  1) *Students need to develop the skill of SOLEs. This took a year with 10-year-old students in Gateshead.*
  2) *Ask students a question such as a GCSE question (one related to the topic of gender and equality from a past paper, for example) to gauge their ability to answer.*

  Evidence has shown that, after the SOLEs skill is developed, they can achieve higher grades when the SOLE method is used as part of standard classroom teaching methods.

- *How can we get more detail out of the students at the presentation stage to prevent the same points being repeated by each group?*

  The ability to swap groups at any point or wander around the room to see what others are finding should, over time, help eliminate this repetition of effort as the students will see what information has already been found and will look for other information.

- *What strategies are there to dissuade a student from working alone rather than in a group?*

  Ask the students to help with this. Perhaps discuss this outside of the SOLE sessions, and ask why, for a few students in our group, the method doesn't seem to work as well as it should. How can we make this better?

Figure 9.2 Benefits and Challenges of SOLEs in England, 2012

Figure 9.3 The School in the Cloud at Newton Aycliffe

All through these years, Katy was helped and encouraged by David Priestly, the head teacher of Greenfield. A handsome and extremely articulate man, David did not fuss over SOLEs, he just watched and came to his own conclusions.

After I won the TED Prize, my discussions with Katy took a new turn.

The School in the Cloud in Greenfield, Newton Aycliffe, was inaugurated on February 13, 2014.

With the new TED Prize funds, Katy built the School in the Cloud in a room opposite the school's reception area; this room had large glass doors and windows on either wall, and the rear wall faced outside the school. The flooring was made of Astroturf™, and this material also covered the tables and computer stations. The whole room looked like a lawn or a park with computers, chairs, and benches. There were cloud-shaped, plastic cutouts on the walls and little rabbits sitting on some of the monitors. There were cloud-shaped pieces of cardboard hanging from the ceiling with questions on them. The room is called Room 13, and it is gorgeous.

Usage of Room 13 was high, and many schools from nearby also booked time to use it. As with the facility in Killingworth, I did not take student assessment measurements in Newton Aycliffe, but I did track the usage over the next three years. The School in the Cloud drew the attention of others. Katy got an offer from a worldwide chain called "Focus Schools" and spent some time in Leamington Spa in the south of England and also in New Zealand and Australia.

Here is her account of those years and Room 13:

SOLE AT GREENFIELD ARTS IN GREENFIELD COMMUNITY COLLEGE

Notes (August 15, 2018):

How Was Room 13 School in the Cloud Lab Used?

We have had 10,710 young people on record in Room 13 exploring SOLE.

This is based on what is recorded to date from 180 sessions. This number doesn't take into account the many sessions facilitated by the Director of Greenfield Arts elsewhere, online, and in training.

An estimate for this is another 100 sessions, and some of those were with large groups, perhaps 30 sessions with 150 participants each for an estimated 670 participants total. It also doesn't include others I have worked with—approximately 600 teachers and 2,500 additional young people.

In total, we expect that we have worked with 14,480 SOLE participants.

Most of the young people were from Greenfield Community College (11–16 years old). We also worked with many primary schools locally and regionally. We had lots of visitors from across the country and globe visiting often. We facilitated SOLE with university students a number of times. We ran community and out-of-school SOLEs. We developed and hosted lots of "training" with educators in Room 13 and also in other schools and organisations regionally.

What Has Happened Since the SOLE Project Finished?

The Director of Greenfield Arts went on secondment (temporary reassignment) from May 2016 to September 2017 and worked on SOLE with 600 UK-based teachers and over 500 in Australia and New Zealand. At Greenfield Community College, local primary schools still book to use the Room 13 space regularly for SOLE. We have worked in addition with all local primary schools in Year 5 and 6 each year through SOLE. Greenfield Community College continues to explore SOLE. A lot of learning has transferred into the classroom and has had an impact on approaches to teaching and learning there. The school was inspected in 2017 by the Office for Standards in Education, Children's Services and Skills (Ofsted) and was judged to require improvement—this has drawn focus on particular school priorities.

Katy is also a regular "Granny" in Noida, India.

What Could Have Been Better?

We could have worked in partnership with Newcastle University to better analyse and understand the information we were gathering and to further explore areas of interest that emerged.

You might be wondering what was behind the Ofsted assessment that the Greenfield Community College required "improvement." Fortunately, this had nothing to do with SOLEs. Around the beginning of 2017, a nearby primary school that was doing poorly was merged into Greenfield. David became the head of the combined school. It was an incredibly challenging task, integrating the two schools and raising the overall standard. At the time of the Ofsted inspection, David had barely begun. The improvement that Ofsted wanted was very much a "work in progress" at the time.

Many TV and press interviews took place in the School in the Cloud at Newton Aycliffe. Among them, an article in *The Guardian* from 2016, titled "The Professor

Link 9.1–9.3:
Articles

Links may also
be accessed at
**resources
.corwin.com/
schoolinthecloud**.

With His Head in the Cloud," covered my emerging experiment—to see if 12-year-olds could answer GCSE questions. It was not a flattering article, decrying the lack of evidence substantiating the effect of SOLEs. Nonetheless, I was undeterred. I did more experiments at Belleville Primary in London and its brilliant principal, John Grove, published a great article on the Belleville School website. He did not present data, just the fact that he saw the children answering GCSE questions in the SOLE, nine years ahead of their time. And then Sarah Leonard, whom you will hear more about later, saw *The Guardian* article. She was livid. Her hard-hitting article in response can be found on the School in the Cloud website. You can read all three articles on the companion website for this book, found at http://resources .corwin.com/schoolinthecloud.

- Link 9.1 Peter Wilby, "Sugata Mitra—The Professor With His Head in the Cloud," *The Guardian*, June 7, 2016.

- Link 9.2 John Grove, "I Don't Need to Know Everything; I Just Need to Know Where to Find It When I Need It," *S.O.L.E.* [Website section].

- Link 9.3 Sarah Leonard, "Urging Students to Teach Themselves," *Positive News*, November 9, 2016.

The way SOLEs should be conducted, in a way that enables 12-year-olds to answer GCSE questions, is just one of the legacies of Room 13. These experiences with SOLEs may not be good enough for *The Guardian*—but they are good enough for me.

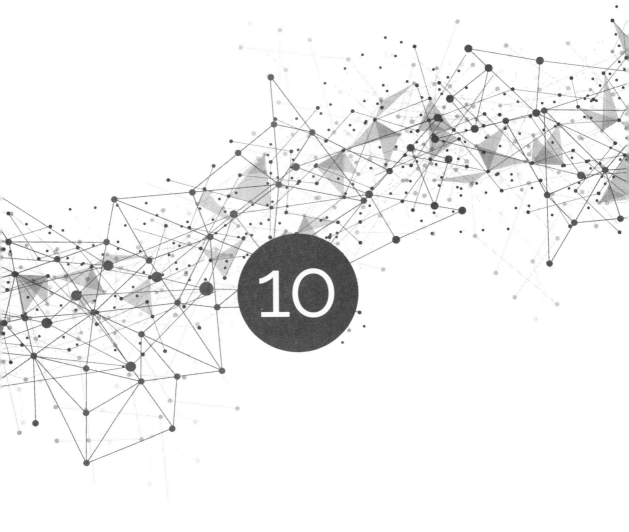

HOW TO BUILD
YOUR OWN SCHOOL
IN THE CLOUD

The seven Schools in the Cloud that we established during the TED project gave us useful data and incredible stories about the impact of the internet on children's learning. There are now many more Schools in the Cloud all over the world. You can find where they are and read their stories by searching online and on the School in the Cloud website: www.theschoolinthecloud.org. You might be inspired to build a School in the Cloud of your own!

On the TED stage in 2013, I admitted, "I don't know how to build a School in the Cloud, because I have never built one." Five years and a million dollars later, this chapter is about how to build a School in the Cloud.

WHY WOULD YOU WANT TO BUILD A SCHOOL IN THE CLOUD?

I hope the stories in this book have given you some answers. To me, the School in the Cloud is insurance against an uncertain future. It is also insulation against the obsolete examination system that is still prevalent today. More practically, the School in the Cloud brings the internet inside the school and the community. If our children are going to live their lives 24/7 with the internet, why should we leave it out of mainstream education?

I think the internet should be a required school subject, like physics or literature. It would of course be challenging to teach. It changes too fast for anyone to write a textbook, and it changes too fast for teachers to keep pace with its current status. Therefore, there would have to be radically different ways for learners to learn about the internet and be evaluated on that learning. You can't teach about the internet, but you can learn about it. From the internet! If you make a meaningful examination about the internet, that examination can only be completed using the internet. And if using the internet, the most important life skill for children today, were to be a subject in school, the School in the Cloud would be the only way for them to learn or be assessed on what they have learned.

Indeed, if school were to be about the biggest questions that humankind faces today, if school were to be about what we don't know, rather than about the long lists of what we do know, the School in the Cloud would be a necessary and vital resource for children.

The internet tells us what humankind knows and where that knowledge is kept, and it brings that knowledge to us in seconds, when and if we need it. It is as if those of us with a smart phone have all the books in the world in our pockets. The internet is changing learning from "just in case" to "just in time." The internet knows what we, in our billions, know and wish to disclose. It does not know things that we know but don't wish to disclose—at least as of 2019. But it is increasingly able to guess things about us that we might not want to disclose or don't even know. It's a bit like a gigantic Sherlock Holmes. We call this AI (artificial intelligence) and are a bit afraid of it, as though it is not made up of humans. But then, we need to realize the internet *is* made up of us.

But of course teachers are still necessary because the internet doesn't know anything about the questions to which no one knows the answers to yet. The teacher who can teach learners how to ask the big questions, to which no one yet knows the answers, will have a steady job for a very long time.

Watch Video 10.1 (Rothwell, 2018) to hear a teacher share why she thinks that the role of a teacher is vital in a SOLE to help children understand how to construct an answer to a really big question.

Video 10.1:
The Role of the
Teacher

Videos may also
be accessed at
**resources
.corwin.com/
schoolinthecloud**.

WILL THE INTERNET EVER BE ALLOWED DURING EXAMINATIONS?

I used to feel depressed about this; it seemed like such a distant and unlikely possibility. Then, about three years ago, I read a news article in India that said that the Indian Army would be deployed to search 300 million children to find and confiscate their smart phones before they entered their examination rooms for high school examinations. Two years later, a similar news item said the children would now be searched for smart phones, smart watches, and wireless earbuds. I felt a wave of irrational joy. In another year or two, children will need to be put through MRI body scanners to check whether they have any means of accessing the internet during examinations. How will exam proctors monitor internet devices that have been surgically implanted?

You cannot keep the internet from entering the examination room. When it does enter, it will destroy the existing assessment system and the teaching methods that cater to it—just as it has destroyed paperbound encyclopedias, the Yellow Pages, paper maps, and a host of other paper-based resources. After generations of teaching with and venerating these resources and the skills needed to navigate them, both the skills and the resources have become obsolete. The principal skills that children need in today's world (who knows about tomorrow?) are using devices, searching the internet, and comprehending the results of their searches.

The School in the Cloud is the solution to this current need. Therefore, if you are an educator, a parent, a community leader, or a concerned citizen, you need to know how to build and operate one.

SPACE

First, you need some space. This could be in a school, a playground, or a community space—in a park or a community library, for example. The space should be in a safe, visible place. You need enough space for about 24 children at a time. Remember the disaster at the Gocharan space, which accommodated 40 children. The smallest amount of space that can hold 24 children is about 25 square meters, or about 225 square feet. The space can be any shape. The smallest I have built is a tiny hexagon in a playground, about which I will tell you later. If you are not short of space, rooms such as the ones in Killingworth or Newton Aycliffe are ideal. They are about 35 square meters, or 300 square feet. I recommend you calculate based on a ratio of 1.5 square meters per child. Out in the open, Korakati is an example of where I got it right, quite by accident.

The walls of the School in the Cloud should have lots of glass, from floor to ceiling, so that the activity inside is clearly visible from the outside. Be careful of echo—there are many inexpensive ways to reduce echo using sound-absorbing material or edges that break up the "standing waves" that make up echoes.

You do need one wall surface that is not glass. This is for a large screen for Skype or other video conferencing or projection. Also, children will need a surface where they can write or pin up things.

You should have as much natural light and fresh air as possible. Direct sunlight on screens can make them harder to read, so you have to find ways to reduce direct sunlight without using curtains. It should be possible to see what is happening inside the School in the Cloud from the outside, and the children inside should know that.

The flooring could be wood, soft tiles, carpet, or that amazing Astroturf™ that Katy put in Newton Aycliffe. Children fall . . . and so do computers. Don't let either get hurt.

FURNITURE

You can use a wall as a writing surface, covered by material on which children can write with erasable pens. Or put in an old-fashioned blackboard with dustless chalk—it looks quaint in the presence of the computers.

If the space is designed for 24 children, you will need six surfaces on which the computer displays can be kept. Use rounded corners on the tables; children in groups can press hard on the tables, trying to look at the screens. In some places, we used semicircular tables while in others, circular tables stretch around pillars that bring the cables down from the ceiling, as in Killingworth. It is much easier to form a group around a circle than along a straight line. The table surfaces should be washable or—even better—writeable. Please do make sure that the legs of the table won't hurt or get in the way of children's legs.

Seating can be in the form of chairs, blocks of foam, or anything light enough for children to move around. This is important because they need to make their own groups and decide where they want to sit in those groups. You can use light stools as well. In Gocharan, we used three-legged stools. The trouble is, the legs would break very easily causing children to fall.

There should be a small table and a chair for the teacher or supervisor to use during SOLE or Granny sessions. A lockable drawer on this table is a good idea. Also, a bit of storage is needed for materials, manuals, paper, spare parts, and so on. A low box that can double as a seat is a possible idea.

COMPUTING EQUIPMENT

This is a hard part to write about, as information will already be obsolete by the time you read it.

Each table needs a large screen, I would say not smaller than 19 inches. In Killingworth, Amy used 29-inch screens. They are marvelous, but expensive. These screens are quite crucial to the functioning of the School in the Cloud.

When we started building the first facilities in India, Ashis and Ranabir used locally fabricated computers, with a floor-standing CPU connected to a screen, keyboard, and mouse. As we saw in Chandrakona, it's easy to steal parts from these CPUs. In Korakati, lizards and snakes made nests inside them, short-circuiting chips in the process. Currently, the computers of choice are all-in-one models where everything is in one single housing attached behind the monitor. Wireless keyboards and mice are available but not advised. Batteries need to be changed often, and the mice can be taken home in a pocket. Also, wireless keyboards and mice can be dropped off the table in a struggle over who should control them. Wired keyboards and mice prevent these problems. Keep the wires long enough so that, when dropped, the keyboard or mouse will simply dangle off the floor.

All computers need to be connected to the internet wirelessly. I know I said the keyboards and mice should be wired, but that is on a table. Ethernet cables for the internet are long and usually run through channels in the floor or ceiling. Mice (as in rodents) like wires. Hence, a wireless router mounted on a wall is the safest option.

A large TV needs to be mounted on a wall for videoconferencing (we use Skype at the moment for this). A web camera should be mounted on top of the TV. The Skype connection can be made from any of the children's computers, but I find it more convenient to have a small laptop for this purpose. The supervisor can use this laptop for her records and mail. The TV should be placed such that, when a session is in progress, the person at the other end should appear life-sized. This is quite important for establishing a realistic presence. It's not very convincing to talk to a postage-stamp-sized face on a tiny screen; likewise, a huge King Kong–like image staring down at children is also not a great idea.

POWER, INTERNET, AND CLIMATE CONTROL

If your School in the Cloud is inside an existing school, you should have power, an internet connection, and some form of climate control already. If you don't, here are some things that may work.

Solar power is getting cheaper and more reliable every year. Ashis installed solar panels in Korakati in 2014, and they are still working fine after four years. The batteries in Korakati are bulky and need to have distilled water topped up every few months. They are very primitive by 2018 standards, but then the so-called "maintenance-free" batteries are much more expensive. The problem is that a solar-powered facility pays for itself over a minimum of 15 years, so the initial investment needs to be large.

I have tried internet connectivity using just about everything I could get. In remote areas like Korakati, we connected using a VSAT dish antenna, directly off a satellite, for over a year. It is incredibly expensive and very slow. The best way to connect is through a service provider (a mobile phone company, for example), and it is wise to get a wireless receiver and a monthly deal for unlimited data usage. This remains expensive in most countries, but India is among the cheapest. In 2018, it is possible to get an unlimited data connection for six computers for around a thousand Indian rupees for a month (in 2019, that equaled US $15 or £10). Children search on YouTube as much or more as they do on search engines such as Google, and this uses up a lot of data.

If you have the power to run an air conditioner, it is advisable in very hot climates, although children living in such places are usually acclimatized to the heat. They can fall sick with air conditioning, so you have to be careful. The same is true with heating in cold climates, although to a lesser extent. The important thing is to ensure enough oxygen and fresh air in the facility.

If your School in the Cloud is in a community setting, you will need a supervisor or coordinator. As I discussed before, parents tend to feel more comfortable with an elderly female supervisor. It is probably best if you can have two people, a man and a woman. The supervisor's job is to look after health and safety. They are *not* required to teach.

Scheduling children's time in a community School in the Cloud is difficult. You may need to develop some kind of a reservation system. Obviously, if there is space available during a time slot and a new child appears, he or she should be let in. Parents should be discouraged from entering the School in the Cloud; they should be encouraged to watch from outside the glass walls.

In a school setting, there should be a reservation system for the School in the Cloud facility. Teachers should be able to book the facility in advance, or use it if it is free during a time slot.

THE DASGHARA MODEL

Dasghara is a village 12 kilometers to the north of the temple city of Tarakeswar in Bengal. It dates back to the early eighteenth century, when a temple to Gupinath (Krishna) was built there (for more information, see the textbox "Gupinath"). The temple is covered in terracotta tiles and is considered one of the finest examples of a terracotta temple, anywhere. The temple was built by one of the ancestors of my mother, Sati Biswas, along with a lake and an imposing mansion. The Biswas family ruled the area for centuries and created the first schools in the region. One of them is a primary school. One of my uncles, Jibanjyoti Biswas, asked me why I was building Schools in the Cloud all over the world but not here, in the village of Gupinath.

So, in the primary school in Dasghara, I built a School in the Cloud, using everything I had learned from building the others during the TED project. It is the last School in the Cloud I have built to date.

GUPINATH

Krishna is the name of a Hindu God of love and compassion. His name is also the word for the colors black or very dark blue. His name appears in Sanskrit literature from the first century BCE and from oral traditions dating to before 2500 BCE. Krishna, in his youth, is famous for his love of Radha, a cowherd. Later in life, Krishna became the charioteer of the warrior Arjun in the battle described in the epic Mahabharata, arguably the longest book in the world. Krishna's planning and political acumen enabled Arjun and his brothers to win the war. In return, they made Krishna the king of Dwarka in the extreme west of India.

The word "gopi" in Sanskrit means "cowherd." The young Krishna was a fabled flautist in addition to his godlike looks. Naturally, he was surrounded by female gopis who literally worshipped him. This resulted in a nickname—Gopinath (the lord of the gopis). This is the name by which he is known all over northern India.

In the east of India, in Dasghara, Bengal, a terracotta temple contains a statue of Krishna playing the flute with Radha by his side. The statue is from the early eighteenth century, as far as I can tell.

The Biswas family of Dasghara owned the temple and the village. They called their god, Gupinath, and the name stuck.

Everyone knows the Gupinath of Dasghara in that region.

I will use the spelling "Gupinath" in this book; I owe that to the school where the Dasghara Model of the School in the Cloud was invented.

The Dasghara School in the Cloud is a hexagonal structure with five glass walls and one brick wall. It is situated on one side of the children's play area. The roof is a flat cone and does not produce any appreciable echo. The flooring is washable and all the furniture, locally made. The whole structure is 5 × 5 meters (about 15 × 15 feet). There is a circular pillar in the center of the structure to support the roof. Three computers are arranged around this pillar, and three more are next to the side walls. The brick wall has a large-screen TV for Skype, and the Wi-Fi receiver is also mounted on this wall. The cost to build this School in the Cloud, from the ground upward and including the structure, computers, furniture, and internet, was £5,000 in 2017 (about 500,000 Indian rupees or US $7,500).

It's a tight squeeze, but the School in the Cloud in Dasghara can hold about 24 children at a time. I think this is the optimal kind of School in the Cloud that a school with limited financial resources can build. I call it the "Dasghara Model."

USING THE SCHOOL IN THE CLOUD

Teachers need to understand what a School in the Cloud is and what to do with it. A three-hour orientation program helps. Get all the teachers together and show

Figure 10.1 The School in the Cloud in Dasghara

them a video on self-organized learning environments (SOLEs). There are many available on the internet, mostly by me. Please don't use the hour-long ones; I cannot understand how anyone can bear them.

There are also other excellent resources on the net, like the video introduction to SOLEs from StartSole (Link 10.1: https://startsole.org). Or you could download a SOLE toolkit from the TED website (Link 10.2: http://media.ted.com/storage/prize/SOLEToolkit.pdf). It's a bit dated, but it has most of the salient features.

Let the teachers discuss the video or ask questions. You may not have the answers, but you can record the questions for the teachers to answer for themselves, later.

Do a demonstration of a SOLE. I find it easiest to do this with a group of about 24 10-year-olds. During the demo, ask the teachers to watch from a distance but to not speak to the children.

Then get the teachers back in discussion mode. They will have questions, comments, suggestions. Tell them they can experiment with the method.

Here is how I would conduct a SOLE session:

CONDUCT A SOLE SESSION

1) Ask the children to sit anywhere they want in the SOLE space. If they are doing this for the first time, they will be curious.

2) Say, "This is a new way to learn. Let's see if it works."

   "Let's see if it works" is something most children like to hear because they can sense that this new way is not a hand-me-down. Children who are used to doing SOLE sessions will not need much instruction or encouragement. They generally love it —if you do it right.

3) Once the children are settled, build up to a question. This is probably the most important part of the session, and it often determines how well the session will go. Refer to examples in this book for guidance in how to build up to a question.

For some additional guidance in forming big questions, view Video 10.2 (Rothwell, 2018) to listen to me thinking through the steps that I take to get to big questions.

Video 10.2:
Big Questions

Example 1: "Can Trees Think?"—Hong Kong, 2011

The TED Global event in Oxford in 2010 is where I first heard Stefano Mancuso. It was one of those rare instances when a talk changed my entire worldview. Mancuso was speaking about trees. He spoke about an experiment he had conducted: in a grove of trees, he inflicted a cut on one tree. The tree started to produce an antibiotic to prevent infection. This was a remarkable feat of nature, but what Mancuso reported next made the audience get very quiet. The other trees in the grove began to produce the antibiotic as well. The wounded tree had warned them through a network of roots and fungi. "An internet under the soil," said Mancuso (2010). To view Mancuso's talk, *The Roots of Plant Intelligence*, visit Video 10.3 on the companion website for this book.

In 2011, I was invited to several international schools in Hong Kong. In one of these, I decided to try to ask the children if trees could think. The session was held in the school library with a few computers scattered on tables. I faced a group of expectant children.

"Do you like trees?" I asked. The children nodded vigorously.

"I love trees too," I said. "They smell nice."

"But there is something really strange about trees, I recently heard."

The children looked at me.

"An Italian scientist said that trees can think."

A buzz and some intakes of breath.

"Now, I don't know what to think about this," I said. "I don't really know that much about trees."

"Shall we try to figure out if trees can think?" I asked, a bit hesitantly.

Video 10.3:
The Roots of Plant Intelligence

Videos may also be accessed at **resources .corwin.com/ schoolinthecloud**.

"'YES!" the children said.

"Well, let's do it this way: you use the internet and discuss among yourselves, and then let's meet again in 40 minutes and see what we think. Shall we?"

The children nodded collectively, looking at each other. I don't think they were used to being allowed to talk.

"You can make your own groups, change groups whenever and if you want to, walk around and see what other groups are doing."

Now the children looked a little alarmed.

"Oh, and one more thing . . . you can't talk to me, and I can't talk to you during the session, so don't ask me anything."

Laughter.

"I am going to need an assistant, to fix problems, you know, because I can't talk to you. You can talk to my assistant, and he or she can talk to me. I can talk to my assistant, and he or she can talk to you."

Bedlam.

A few minutes of loud discussions later, the children chose an assistant for me, an Indian boy they thought would make a good manager.

The SOLE began.

It took about 10 minutes for the children to get into the spirit of the SOLE. Then there was the familiar humming noise that I had heard so many times at the Hole-in-the-Wall sites. Then came rapid movement across computers and vehement conversation. My assistant was busy fixing computers and disputes.

"Can I go to the bathroom?" asked a child.

My assistant stepped in. "Thirty seconds," he said, holding up his watch.

I must tell you that toward the end of the 40 minutes, my assistant was found prone on the ground with two boys holding him down. His shoes had been confiscated. "Well, better him than me," I thought.

The watching teachers could barely hold themselves back from stepping in during these 40 minutes, but I held up a warning finger.

"We don't have any more time," I said, at the end of the 40 minutes. "Tell me what you found."

The children told us that, in their opinion, trees cannot think. "Exchanging chemicals may be clever, but it is not the same as thinking or communicating," they said. It was, indeed, the collective scientific opinion of that time—comprehended by 12-year-olds in 40 minutes.

The teachers asked me later how they could have understood the meaning of research papers in journals. Their reading skills are just not enough for that. Well, you know how that works by now, don't you?

Example 2: "Can Trees Think?"—Bristol, 2018

In July 2018, I tried the same question I had asked in Hong Kong seven years earlier. This time it was a primary school in Bristol and a group of about 20 children, 11 years old.

It had been a long, hot summer in England. You don't have to believe me, but you should; it really was a very hot summer. The school I was in had a room specially built for SOLEs. I was absolutely delighted to see that.

"I live in the north, in Gateshead," I said, after introducing myself.

"You know it was so hot up there, the ground was beginning to turn brown and the trees looked pale and tired."

The children nodded grimly.

"But I noticed that the young trees, which had grown from the seeds dropped by the older trees, were looking greener and fresher in the shade of their parents."

The children looked at me, I think they had not heard of trees being referred to as parents.

"But then, you know, the amount of water available in the ground is about the same everywhere, so where were the young trees getting more water from?"

Silence.

"Could it be, the older trees were passing the water available to the younger trees, instead of using it themselves?" I asked, in a low voice.

The children leaned forward, murmuring.

"Can trees think, can they talk to each other, can they decide to do things?"

Silence.

"I don't really know the answer; shall we try to find out?"

Vigorous nodding.

I then told them about making groups, talking, walking around, and all the "non-rules" of the SOLE. I told them they could not talk to me. These children had done this before—they understood.

"I need an assistant." Many hands went up.

"Wait," I said, "you can't vote for yourself—you have to tell me who, other than yourself, will make the best assistant."

Confusion, argument, and the politics of healthy democracy followed. A little girl was chosen as my assistant. Later, the teachers told me this little girl spent most of her time telling other people what to do. She was very good at that. We might be looking at a great future leader here.

The SOLE began.

That day, in Bristol, the children reported about cells at the tip of root fibers in plants that look and behave like neurons. The root system is like a neural network—a brain. The brains communicate chemically with each other through microscopic, thread-like fungi. The trees communicate. They have been evolving for longer than humans have. Parent trees give up their water and nutrients for the babies, even if they, the parents, have to die.

It was only seven years since Hong Kong, seven years of research, summarized by the voices of children. Stefano Mancuso, whose work I was so impressed by years ago in the Oxford TED, would have been proud. SOLEs can bring in the latest research findings to children, before their "official" curricula catch up.

A small boy looked back through the school window at a grove of trees just behind the playground.

"They can think," he whispered.

Example 3: "The Reconstruction of Japan"

In an international school in Singapore, I had just finished talking about SOLEs with the teachers. We were discussing what might be an interesting SOLE to do. These were the days when, in England, Emma and I were experimenting with what 8-year-olds might do with GCSE A-Level questions. The teachers in Singapore were interested. One of them said he was working with final year students (about 17 years old) on a question about the U.S. reconstruction of Japan after the World War II. We decided to try this question with 12-year-olds. I must have been in a very adventurous mood because I suggested we do the same question with 7-year-olds as well. The teachers were a bit astounded, and, I must confess, I too was rather alarmed by what came out of my mouth.

We formed two groups: one consisting of 24 14-year-olds and the other of about 16 7-year-olds. They were in two different spaces. I went to the younger group first.

"Many years ago, there was a great war. People were fighting all over the world."

The children listened eagerly.

"The Americans invented a huge weapon, the atomic bomb, and dropped it on Japan."

"The war ended after that, but Japan had to be repaired because everything was broken by the American bomb."

The children nodded vigorously with serious faces, as though they always repair anything they have broken.

"So, shall we find out how the Americans reconstructed Japan after World War II?"

Yes.

"Well, I don't quite know what they did. Will you find out from the internet?"

After the usual explanation of the SOLE setup, they began, and I left for the room where the older children were.

"You know about World War II don't you?" I asked.

They said they did.

"So, how did it end?"

"The Germans lost," one of them said.

"Do you know what happened to Japan during the war?" I asked.

They knew about Pearl Harbor and about Hiroshima but not much about what happened in between. A few had been to the military museum on Sentosa Island but remembered little.

"You know, there is a question in the national A-Level examination. It says to write a paragraph on the reconstruction of Japan after World War II."

"It's meant for 17-year-olds, but do you think you could try it, if you could discuss among yourselves and use the internet?"

They looked at me, incredulously. "Yes," they said, with no hesitation at all.

I explained the methodology of the SOLE, got my assistant, and the SOLE began.

Half an hour later, the 14-year-olds gave a meticulous account of General McCarthy's reconstruction policies in Japan, the rules he made, the final freedom of Japan, and the end of the occupation. It was, according to the teacher, a good answer and would get them a great grade in the A-Level exam. He was really pleased.

"Fantastic!" I told the children. "You did a remarkable job answering a question meant for 17-year-olds."

"Those 17-year-olds must be really stupid," said one of the girls.

Everybody giggled.

The 7-year-olds had finished and gone off to play. I got them back.

"So, what did you find out about the reconstruction of Japan?" I asked in a very academic voice with my glasses low on my nose. They laughed.

One of them spoke.

"America won, and Japan lost. So the Americans told the Japanese how bad they [the Japanese] were. Then they told the Japanese what to do to fix everything that was broken. Then when everything was fixed the Japanese told them how good they [the Japanese] were."

"Em . . . ," I spluttered. It seemed to me that the answer was remarkably accurate in a 7-year-old kind of way.

Everybody clapped.

Example 4: "How Do the Physical and Climactic Conditions We Have in Australia Affect the Way We Live?"

In St. Aidan's in Gateshead, Emma once did a SOLE with Year 4 and Year 5 children (9- to 10-year-olds). She used a simple trick to ask a not too interesting geography question. She got our friend Brett Millott of Melbourne to record a question on video and send it to her. Then she projected the video on the wall. The children had no clue about what Brett was saying in his Australian accent. But Brett had anticipated this, and the question was written on a board next to his head.

"How do the physical and climactic conditions we have in Australia affect the way we live?" was the question.

"Let's read this question very carefully," said Emma, and read it out to them, slowly.

What followed was a classic SOLE. The children took time—after all they had no idea what "climactic" meant. And many of them had no idea what was on the other side of the Tyne River, let alone on the other side of the world.

This question was tackled by the two different groups (Year 4 and Year 5), simultaneously.

The children reported on how the central deserts of Australia made people live around the edges of the continent. The students also discovered that there were people living in the center of Australia in a place called Coober Pedy who lived underground because of the extreme heat. They showed clear comprehension. You can view this SOLE in action by clicking on the QR code and watching Video 10.4 on YouTube.

You will notice in the video that the person whom I refer to as "my assistant" used to be called a policeman. This works well in England where the PC, or police constable, is a friendly, reassuring figure who is, nevertheless, to be obeyed.

Not so in Australia. Brett and Paul put an end to the policeman role in SOLEs. Their reasoning was that a "policeman" role for one or two students was not supportive of the self-organizing philosophy and that it just transferred the traditional power role within the classroom or session from the teacher to a student. So I changed the name of the role to "assistant."

Video 10.4:
Australian
Climate

Videos may also
be accessed at
**resources
.corwin.com/
schoolinthecloud**.

CREATING AND POSING BIG QUESTIONS

From these examples, you might begin to see how questions are built and posed. There is really no method for creating a question. You can find lists of questions at startsole.org. In the end, though, the question has to come from you, in your own words. One way to get to a "good" question is to ask a series of questions to yourself about the topic you are dealing with. For example, if your topic is "The Roman Empire," you might proceed to think like this:

1. Why should children know about the Roman Empire? Because it is an important part of human history.

2. Why should children know about human history? Because it explains many things about the way we are today.

3. Why should children know about what we are like? Because they must understand what it means to be human.

4. Why should children know what it means to be human? Because they must understand their reality.

5. Why should children understand reality? Hmmm. . . .

So my favorite question, from a 5-year-old, is "Are we real?"

Go ahead and think all this through. Maybe you could show them a picture of the Colosseum in Rome and ask, "What is that building, and why is it broken?"

Maybe they will reach an understanding of their reality that way.

Once you have built up to the question, the SOLE can start. Move out of the way and watch from some distance. This is the children's research time. Use your assistant for any help that you may need. The assistant can help you with most things—from sorting out disagreements to getting isolated children into groups, cheering everybody up, and whatever else may come up during the session.

Sessions can have various durations, depending on what you want to achieve. With very young children, say below 8 years old, it may be prudent to keep the duration of the researching to about 30 minutes or less. Most SOLE sessions should not be more than 45 minutes long. You can tell when the session is coming to a close when you notice children getting restless or too quiet, or chatting.

When you think it is right, get the children to come back to the "class" mode. Have them present their results. I don't recommend having every child present. This takes too long and gets boring. Have the children present in groups. Now, you might wonder how to ensure that every child has learned individually. You can't— any more than if you were "teaching" a traditional class. In any learning situation, you get some learners who get it all, some who don't have a clue, and most who get it more or less. This is called a Gaussian distribution, and it is the reason exam scores always show up on graphs in a bell-shaped curve.

There is another problem with group presentations.

Remember groups are meant to be fluid and transient. The teacher doesn't form the groups, the children do, and they can change groups when they like. My solution is to tell the children that we will have as many presentations as there are computers. This ensures that they will present in groups of approximately four. Each group should be given just a few minutes to present its findings. Suggest that groups presenting later should not repeat things that other groups have already said, as this will waste time. Tell them that, by the time the students of the last groups present, other groups might have said everything they wanted to say. There is no problem with that—they should simply say they had also come across what the others had.

When one group is presenting, others should listen. Tell them that if they don't listen to others, then, when their turn comes, others may not listen to them. Tell them to speak slowly and clearly. This is good practice in public speaking for them. Encourage them to acknowledge each other's work. "I found this out from another group" is a marvelous outcome, if you can get it. At the end of each presentation, there should be applause, just like in a conference.

Now comes the hardest part of a SOLE for you, the teacher. Putting it all together.

Listen to the first presentation and summarize it. For example, you might say, "Very good. The first group has found that the Colosseum was like a stadium for games. But they added, the games could be very violent, with people killing each other and animals. My goodness!"

Then listen to the next group and find a way to tie in the content with that presented by the earlier group. For example, "The second group has added something very important to what the first group said. They said that gladiators were mostly slaves, and they didn't really want to fight. It's just that they had no choice because the Romans were powerful and had conquered their countries."

Move on the next group and so on. At the end, summarize everything. I *never* "value add." I simply say, this is what you found, and it was really impressive given the short time—or something positive like that. I tell them there are many things they found that I did not know. You will find that this is true for most SOLEs. If there are things the children have left out, don't fill in the gaps. Frame another question for another SOLE later. The children will realize they had left something out the previous time.

SOLEs don't need to be done every day. Some teachers say once a week for each class is good enough. Some teachers say they start a topic with a SOLE and then teach normally—frequently referring to what students discovered in it. "Just as you found out in the SOLE . . ." and so on. Some teachers end a topic with a SOLE to explore the more advanced or esoteric aspects of that topic.

In one school, the teacher starts by describing what she is planning to do on a particular day. She told me that, on some days, the children would say, "Why don't we just SOLE that?" On other days, they might say, "You tell us . . . it will take too long to find out." I think this is so healthy—the learners and the teacher together deciding on a pedagogy.

If a teacher is absent, a substitute teacher or the principal can call the absent teacher and ask for a good question. Then do a SOLE on this. Tell the children, "Look, Mr. X is absent, and I have no idea about the subject, but this is the question he suggested." I have done SOLEs on subjects I had no idea about, in a language I don't know (Spanish), using the children's minds and Google translate!

Most teachers, and some data, tell me that children remember everything they did in a SOLE for years. Why? They found it all by themselves and were congratulated for doing so.

WHEN SOLES GO WRONG

Self-organized learning environments are delicate things to set up. They can go wrong for all sorts of reasons. Here are two examples.

Example 1: Avoid the Possibility of a Student Working Alone

In a school in the UK, 10-year-olds were working on the question "How do fish swim so fast?"

Everything seemed to be going smoothly until the time came for the children to present. Several groups talked about how the shape of fish help them glide easily through water, how their tails can be used to propel them forward and also act as rudders to change direction, how the fins maintain balance, and so on. I was getting impressed and happy when a little girl spoke with some agitation. She said sharks were killed for their skins, and these were used to make swimsuits so that people could swim faster. She had run across the term "sharkskin swimsuits." She had not realized that "sharkskin" fabric is artificial and has no relationship to real sharks and their skins. The other children looked horrified. I was alarmed but ended the session by summarizing what everyone had said and adding, "It would be really bad if we killed sharks for their skins. We really must find out more about this."

So what went wrong? This girl had not been working in a group. There were too many computers in the room, and she had been working on a computer alone. SOLEs need to be set up with a few computers with large screens so that children can work in self-organized, fluid groups. I cannot emphasize this enough.

Example 2: Allot Enough Time

In a school in Singapore, the teachers said the children were not interested in English literature. I struck up a loose conversation about Shakespeare. The children made faces.

"Well, I believe Shakespeare said some really funny things, sometimes a bit naughty too," I said.

I asked the children if they would like to find some funny lines from Shakespeare in 20 minutes.

While they started a bit reluctantly, soon I could hear the girls giggling as they encountered the bawdy stuff. The SOLE warmed up, and the boys started laughing too. They started to run around looking at each other's lines.

After the 20 minutes were up, the children were deep in their search, but I had to wrap things up, as there was no time left.

"Who can tell me the funniest line?" I asked.

'I would challenge you to a battle of wits, but I see you are unarmed,' said a boy, and everybody, including the teachers watching, started laughing.

"We love the way he writes," said some children, to the amazement of the English teacher.

But all was not well. Later, in my hotel room, I discovered that Shakespeare had not written that line about the battle of wits.

So what went wrong? I think it was the timing of the SOLE. You have to give each SOLE enough time. If the children are engaged and still working, it means the SOLE has not come to its logical end. In this case, 20 minutes was way too short a period of time. The groups had no time to self-correct. They came to a wrong conclusion.

When such errors happen, you can correct them with a subsequent SOLE. It does not help at all to point out to the children that they made a mistake. They must discover the mistake themselves and correct it. Pointing out mistakes leaves bad memories behind. That is not what schools are for.

You can help the children find their mistakes by posing other questions that will show them the mistakes. This is how we catch mistakes in scientific research where there is nobody to "point out" a mistake.

The School in the Cloud is like a spaceship in internet space, with the children at the controls. The teacher is there as their friend, not their guide, because, often, the teacher doesn't know where they are going to go. Teachers ask me what their role is in self-organized learning. I can only summarize with one line:

"You go there; I will go with you."

GLIMPSES OF THE
FUTURE OF LEARNING

PART III

WHAT DID WE LEARN
FROM THE SCHOOLS
IN THE CLOUD?

HOW MUCH CAN WE RELY
ON RESEARCH?

Should you research first, develop a theory, and then create a new model? I think you could, but you may end up with a "solution in search of a problem."

If you have a problem, you should solve it; few would argue about that.

A long time ago, it was a problem to carry coal up to the top of a mine in a colliery. George Stephenson solved this problem by improving upon the steam engines and the locomotives already in use at the collieries of his day. Stephenson's machine was huge, at first, and sat on top of the colliery, pulling a rope tied to wagons of coal that moved up a track. Then he made the engine small enough to mount on to one of the wagons so that the whole thing, engine and all, could move along the track. No one understood how it worked, but the coal went up the slope to where it had to go. When he first demonstrated it, people said, "It will never start." Then, when his engine, the *Rocket* as it was called, started to roll, they said, "It will never stop." Scientists began to search frantically for how the steam engine worked. A new branch of physics called thermodynamics was discovered and went on to change our view of the entire universe!

Stephenson solved the problem first; the research came later.

While cooking, if you invent a new recipe that tastes rather nice, you should publish it. People will then tell you why it will never work, why you should have measured different amounts of each ingredient against a "control" and proved that it will work, before you go around claiming that it does. The proof of the pudding, it seems, is not in the eating. Social science can be a bit like that.

In an article called "The Problem With 'Show Me the Research' Thinking," Rick Wormeli (2018) quotes Walt Gardner:

> [I]nvestigators pore over data previously collected by others. They seek correlations between different variables. . . . The trouble is that observational studies are subject to biases that sometimes make the results unreliable. If results can't be replicated by others, the conclusions lose credibility.

Link 11.1:
"The Problem With 'Show Me the Research' Thinking" Article (Wormeli, 2018)

Links may also be accessed at **resources .corwin.com/ schoolinthecloud**.

Wormeli concludes, "Though we might lack the tools to get it right every time, we are attentive to others' research while contributing research of our own. We make the most conscientious decision we can, given our growing expertise and the context of any given moment. For most of us, that'll do." You can read the whole article on the companion website (see Link 11.1).

In *Visible Learning for Teachers*, John Hattie (2012) says that collective teacher efficacy (CTE) is ranked as the number one factor influencing student achievement. What is CTE? It is the shared belief among teachers that, through their collective action, they can have a positive influence on student outcomes. When teachers believe in a method, they can make it work. Collective teacher efficiency (CTE) can solve the problem before the research catches up. Groups of teachers can collectively reproduce each other's results. They are doing good science, even if they don't think of it that way.

This book cites research that is peer reviewed, award winning, and published in some of the best journals in the world. This book also includes research that is based on small samples, published in somewhat obscure journals. Furthermore, there is anecdotal data from teachers all over the world. There are stories from children. There is also unpublished work that I did not want to hold back from you. In the end, the proof of my pudding will be in your eating. I hope you don't mind.

WHAT DID WE LEARN FROM THE SCHOOLS IN THE CLOUD?

Since 1999, the Hole-in-the-Wall and SOLEs ventures and the Schools in the Cloud have provided us with a rich source of data, observations, stories, and debates. Is there a central message that is evident in these years of excitement? Are there significant lessons for educators in our experiences?

A thunderstorm broke over Gateshead after a long and hot summer as I began to write this chapter. Then the air became still again—fresh and crystal clear.

Using Technology

We know that children can learn to use devices on their own. They can learn even faster in unsupervised groups. So that means we don't need to waste time "introducing" them to most new technology. Just leave them alone to figure it out. Once in a while, they might break something; account for that in your maintenance costs. If you assign them the task of teaching adults how to use the new technology, they will be very happy and even more engaged with learning it. Recall that we discussed in Chapter 1, how children showed a steady growth in digital literacy over time with no teacher intervention (Figure 1.2 is reproduced here as Figure 11.1.)

So what does this unsupervised acquisition of digital literacy tell us? To me, it shows us a generation that can use any digital technology to solve problems. They can *compute* the solutions to problems—compute as in put a solution together with the resources available. They don't create solutions; they compute solutions. Computing is the new arithmetic.

Reading Comprehension

We know that reading comprehension improves when children use the School in the Cloud. Our data show that groups of children trying to figure things out for themselves on the internet learn to read and understand content at an accelerated rate. It is important to note that "reading comprehension" is only one of the factors in understanding content. In addition to printed text, children also reference many other types of media including visual representations, audio, and video. The data on "reading comprehension" in this book should really be read as "multimedia comprehension." A consistent data finding throughout all of the School in the Cloud sites has been that comprehension improves at levels above that which we have seen with standard instruction.

Figure 11.2 shows a scatterplot representing the reading comprehension scores over time from four sites (Korakati, Chandrakona, Kalkaji, Phaltan). The growth shows a steady increase in levels of reading comprehension.

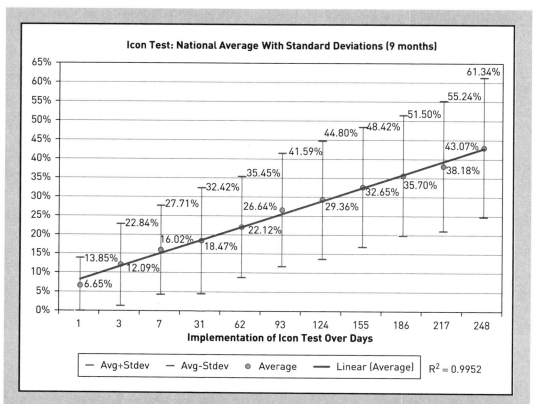

Figure 11.1 Growth in Computer Literacy Over a Nine-Month Period

Source: Mitra et al. (2005). *Australasian Journal of Educational Technology,* Vol. 21, No. 3.

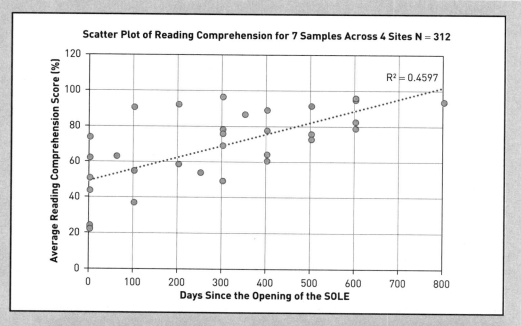

Figure 11.2 Reading Comprehension Improvement Across Four Sites

From the study in Phaltan, described in Chapter 7, we know that this improvement in reading comprehension is more than what we could expect through traditional schooling during the same period.

Phaltan also showed us that children as young as six can participate in the School in the Cloud. They can't read well at all, but they find pictures and videos to learn what they are looking to know. In the process, they somehow start to read. More evidence of very young children learning how to read in SOLEs came from the Sidhuwal site.

In 2018, Ritu built a School in the Cloud in a village called Sidhuwal, deep in heart of rural Punjab. Here, she let 5-year-olds in. The children knew virtually no English and could barely identify the English and Punjabi alphabets. The teachers were not much better, I am afraid.

Ritu measured reading comprehension over a two-month period, about once every 10 days. By the end of the second month, the children were beginning to read and speak a few sentences. See Figure 11.3.

We can't really conclude anything from this tiny experiment—it's merely a rather tantalizing hint—but the rest of the data is clearer: children learn to read faster and better in the School in the Cloud. It is perhaps possible to start with children as young as five years old.

Here is a generation that can comprehend the world from the massive cloud of data surrounding them. *Comprehension* is the new reading.

Internet Searching Skills

We know that groups of children researching on the internet get better at searching for things and usually detect errors in information or their perceptions. If we draw a scatterplot of their internet searching skills across all the sites where we could measure, we can see this improvement visually (Figure 11.4).

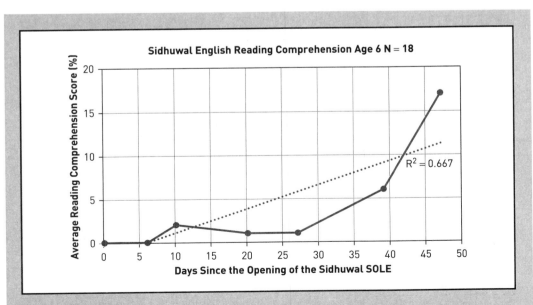

Figure 11.3 Sidhuwal: Reading Comprehension Improvement in 6-Year-Olds, 2018

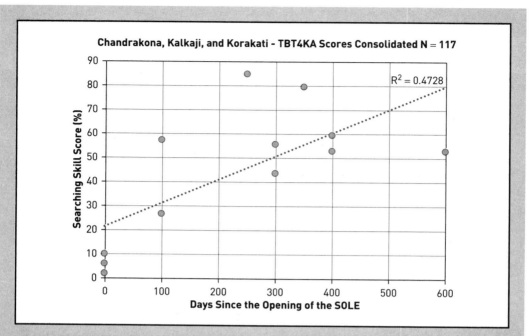

Figure 11.4 Internet Searching Skills of Children at Chandrakona, Kalkaji, and Korakati

In Figure 11.4, you can clearly see the Kalkaji girls' data (the three dots way over the line) soaring over the results from the other two sites. But then those girls had already been in SOLEs for about six months when we began collecting the data.

In order to show a more realistic picture, I used the same reasoning as I had with Suneeta's data for Phaltan. Since the Kalkaji girls were already ahead of the children at Chandrakona and Korakati, we should compare their scores with the scores at Chandrakona and Korakati *after* six months. One way to do this would be to add six months (I added 200 days) to the dates of measurements at Kalkaji. We would then be comparing the scores at all three places after approximately the same durations of usage. This gives us what is shown in Figure 11.5.

We see the regression (how closely the line fits the data) in Figure 11.5 improve quite dramatically. The girls' scores at Kalkaji had predicted what the scores in the other two Schools in the Cloud would be, six months later.

Within approximately six months, children using the School in the Cloud learn how to search better on the internet. This should perhaps be obvious since online searching is usually not a subject taught in schools, particularly primary schools. Unlike in traditional schools, in SinCs, children learn to research in groups, correct each other, and discuss which findings are more authentic. In doing so, children learn to communicate with the network, ask the right questions (in the right way), and explain and discuss their findings with each other.

Communication is the new writing.

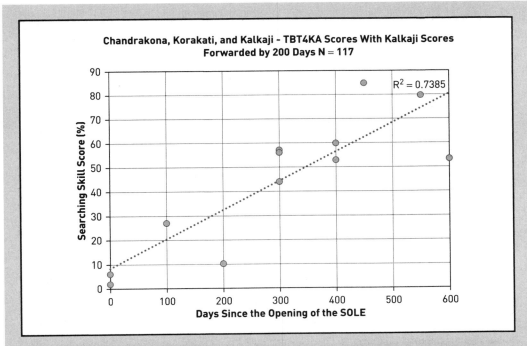

Figure 11.5 Internet Searching Skills of Children at Chandrakona, Kalkaji, and Korakati, With Kalkaji Scores Adjusted

Self-Confidence

When children research on the internet and are congratulated on their achievements, it is natural to expect that their confidence in themselves will improve. I expected our measurements of self-confidence to show this improvement.

The self-confidence measurements were surprising to me. Figure 11.6 tells us that there is not such a great improvement in scores. Suneeta had expected this finding. The children were quite self-confident to start with—scoring between 3 and 4.5 on a 5-point scale (a score of 5 indicates that the observer strongly agrees with the statement, "This child is high on confidence"). And that self-confidence remained high through the period of measurement, neither increasing nor decreasing by any significant amount. Here I need to point out that the self-confidence we are looking at is with reference to internet access and researching. We may not have seen the same confidence if we were dealing with Sanskrit or Latin poetry recital.

Here is a generation that is confident of its digital skills. The children are not afraid of modern technology; they only need access to it. The results of the 1999 Hole-in-the-Wall experiments had, like a weathervane, pointed at this.

A great statement of hope!

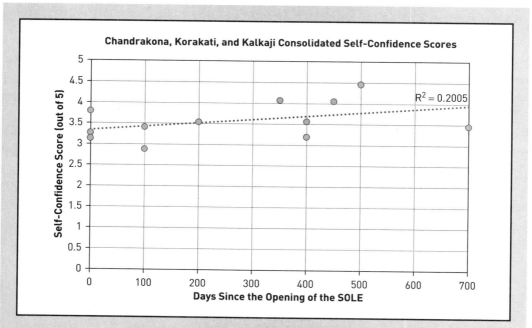

Figure 11.6 Self-Confidence Scores for Chandrakona, Kalkaji, and Korakati

In the end, the Hole in the Wall and the School in the Cloud were showing us that there had been a fundamental change in the skills children need for the times in which they are growing up.

A transition had occurred, a movement from reading, writing, and arithmetic to comprehension, communication, and computing.

IS NO PEDAGOGY
GOOD PEDAGOGY?

Minimally Invasive Education

do not have a formal background in education. I studied physics at university, and went on to a PhD in the theoretical physics of organic semiconductors. But don't throw this book into the bin (garbage, for my American friends) yet.

I became involved in education for several reasons. In the 1970s, I started writing for a children's magazine called *Target* because I needed the money. I wrote about the latest findings in science and the editor, Rosalind Wilson, thought I wrote well and understood how children learned. Encouraged, I even started writing poems for children. I hoped these poems might make children ask questions and look for answers. I never got to publish any because Rosalind died. Devastated, I stopped writing. Here is the last poem that Rosalind and I laughed about together:

On our way to Dehradoon,

we cross the plains at last.

As we climb into the Shivaliks,

we climb into the past.

And if the brown and green hills

look scary from the bus. . . .

Remember, it's the land

Of the Ramapithecus.

(*Ramapithecus punjabicus*, now known as the *Sivapithecus*, roamed the foothills of the Shivalik mountains in the Himalayas 14 million years ago. Dehradoon, now usually spelled as Dehradun, is the capital of the Indian state of Uttarakhand, near the Himalayan foothills.)

Decades later, in 1999, the Hole-in-the-Wall project put me back firmly into children's education.

EDUCATION

Everyone seems to know what education is, and no one seems to be able to articulate it. Is it so abstract that words fail us?

I want to try to find out what education might be. Reading is not getting me anywhere, so let us go at it *ab initio* (from first principles). That's allowed in physics. Let's go there, then, and hope that Aristotle, Tagore, and Piaget will come with us.

A newborn baby is not educated, unless there is some "education" inside its genes. There is some work that says that memories and some learning from the past can reside in genes, but there isn't enough data at this time for us to work with that information. Instead, let's say that the baby has some instincts—programs that are wired into its genes from a long time ago—like how to breathe or make a noise.

The baby's actions are not based on memories of the past or anticipation of the future. It breathes not because it has breathed before and not because it will breathe again. It breathes in the "now." It cries not because it has cried before and not because it anticipates any result from its crying. It cries in the "now."

And then, things happen. It feels better when it breathes, better than when it doesn't. It now breathes, with the memory of having breathed before and in the anticipation of feeling better. When it cries, things happen—sometimes food appears, sometimes soothing words. It cries, with the memory of past gratification, in the anticipation of something pleasurable that will happen.

It tosses its arms and legs about. They disappear and reappear from view. Quite predictably. It repeats its actions, checking its predictions against its memory of past actions. It checks this over and over again.

Its education has begun.

Our chain of thinking seems to lead us toward a view of education that changes human action from instantaneous and situational to more "informed." Each action considers memory of the past and anticipation of the future. Using this view, it becomes easy to see that the process of education should

1. improve knowledge of the past, and how to use that knowledge, and

2. improve the ability to anticipate possible futures.

Is that all there is to education? This seems very simplistic, but sometimes nature prefers the simple alternative. A few examples might help. Let's continue with our *ab initio* thinking.

1. You are visiting a country you have never been to before. An elderly woman on a bus smiles at you and asks you to vacate your seat. Should you do so? Should you refuse? Should you ask others around what to do? Why is she asking you to do this? What will happen if you do or don't? To answer these questions, you would need knowledge of the past of the country and of its people and culture. This knowledge would also help you work out the possible outcomes in the future.

2. You want to build a school and have located an excellent building that is for sale. You don't have the funds to buy it outright. A charitable trust offers to help fund your project in return for a stake in the proposed school. Alternatively, you could try to get a mortgage from a bank. What should you do? In order to make a decision, you will need to know the history of the charitable trust and of trusts in general in the country. You will need to know what impact a "stake in the school" might have on your project. It will help if you know the history and background of the person offering. For the bank option, you will need to know about interest rates and their history in the country, the trends in the national economy, the past reputation of the bank, and so on. All this will help you to figure out the possible outcomes of your decision.

3. You need to replace a switch for an electric shower in your bathroom. It is mounted on the ceiling and operated with a pull chord. What should you do? Should you do it yourself? What do most people do in this

situation in your neighborhood? Should you call an electrician to do this? Are electricians reliable? If you have to do this yourself, where do people buy switches? What are the colors of the live, neutral, and earth wires? Should you switch the mains off? If you think about it, all these questions have their answers in knowledge of the past—from the reliability of local electricians to the workings of electricity. You need that information to figure out what the consequences of your decision might be.

4. Your colleague at work says he is not feeling well. What should you do? Your decision will depend on your knowledge of your colleague's habits, health, age, and similar information that will help you figure out what the possible consequences of not feeling well could be. Accurate knowledge of the past and the ability to imagine the right possible futures will be essential for you to act.

You can create hypothetical examples for yourself, and, I think, in every case you will find that you need knowledge from or of the past and the ability to assemble that knowledge into possible future options.

If this is what education is about, then schools should be designed for it. And indeed, that is so. If you look at any curriculum, you will notice it will try to introduce you to all sorts of things, just in case they come in handy. As we saw in earlier chapters, this method is not very practical or useful anymore. In today's world (and presumably tomorrow's), you need to be able to figure things out in the moment based on a given need. Consider the four examples above. In each case, being able to explore those questions on the internet would be immensely helpful in making a sound and informed decision.

EDUCATION AND COGNITION

If we allow a child to grow up with no formal education at all, that child will still learn continuously from its own experience and surroundings. So is the process of education aimed at "stretching" our knowledge of the past and using that knowledge to better estimate the future? The process of education could then be described as "any process that increases cognitive ability in brains."

> **Education is any process that improves the ability to act by using knowledge of or from the past in combination with and directed toward one or many imagined futures.**

If we add to this that cognitive ability uses knowledge of the past and the ability to look at the future as its basis, we might define education in the following words: Education is any process that improves the ability to act by using knowledge of or from the past in combination with and directed toward one or many imagined futures.

There can be instances when the past influences your actions more than the future. There can be instances when past influences and future anticipations work at the same intensity, such as when you are jostled in a bar while carrying a drink, teeter for a bit, but don't spill a drop. In an instant, your brain uses your knowledge (formally learned or otherwise) of hydrodynamics and gravity. It anticipates the consequences, financial and social, of spilling a drink. It acts.

There are instances when future anticipation overrides the past, such as when you buy stock for a miserably performing company making driverless cars.

In order to educate our children, we need to let them understand and use the past, as well as to see and use an anticipated future.

USING THE PAST

The curriculum in schools is mostly about the past. It is about everything we, humanity, already know. We box all this knowledge into subjects and pour information into our children's minds. A teacher in India once described this approach to me as the "Jug-Mug" model. The child's mind is an empty mug into which the teacher pours knowledge from a full jug. It works. That's how my mug got filled.

But what if, instead of lots of jugs of knowledge, there was a vast lake, and the children could just fill their mugs from that themselves?

The jug-mug model is from a time when that lake did not exist. It exists now, and everyone can draw from it who has access to the internet. If you can't reach deep enough, your friends can help you.

Julie Stern explains a similar analogy for learning in her book *Tools for Teaching Conceptual Understanding, Secondary: Designing Lessons and Assessments for Deep Learning.*

> In the traditional model of learning, students play a rather passive role, waiting for the teacher to point out the facts and ideas they should "collect" in their jars. The goal of this type of learning is for students to hold all the facts in their heads until the end of the year (or until the day of the test), at which point they dump out the ideas they have learned to prove they have retained them. This type of learning does not invite students to shape the ideas or construct their own meaning; rather, students' minds are seen as empty jars waiting to be filled with the ideas of others. (Stern, Ferraro, & Mohnkern, 2017, p. 35)

This model of learning is depicted in a student drawing found in Stern's book (see Figure 12.1).

Let's take some examples.

If a small steel ball fell from about 10 centimeters above onto the back of your palm, it would hurt less than if a rubber ball had fallen from a meter above. But if the same steel ball had fallen from a meter above, it would have hurt a lot

Figure 12.1 The Empty Jar Model of Learning

Source: Stern, Ferraro, & Mohnkern (2017). Jimmy Conde, graphic artist. Reprinted with permission.

more than the rubber ball. The physics of why this is so has been known for over 300 years, and it is useful to know. You can use this knowledge to work out what to throw at whom and from what height.

To test if you know this fact, a good question might be the following: "If a steel ball and a rubber ball of the same size fall on your hand from a great height, the impact of the steel ball hurts more. Why is this so?"

Unfortunately, this question is not what is asked in most examinations. Instead the question might be the following: "A steel ball of mass 200 grams is dropped from a height of 1 meter. At what velocity will it hit the ground?"

Your phone can calculate that easily, if you know how to ask it. Being able to calculate the velocity is not as important as knowing *why* the velocity is more or less depending on the height from which the ball is dropped. *Why* is "impact" more when the velocity is more? These questions are usually not asked.

Here's another example.

A statue was found in the archaeological site of the Indus Valley civilization, in the ruins of one of the earliest cities in the world, Mohenjo-Daro (see Figure 12.2). It was made about 5,000 years ago. It is the statue of a confident young woman in a dancing pose. Who were the people who made it, and why did they make it?

An answer to this question requires knowledge of the past, what art is, why a society invests in art, and what money and time have to do with art. Perhaps even what an affluent society is. Answering this question may help you understand art in contemporary society and how art might develop in the future.

Figure 12.2 The Dancing Girl of Mohenjo-Daro

Most examinations will not ask this question. Instead they will ask if you know the date of the statue, when it was found, and by whom. Examinations are boring and factual for a reason.

ASSESSMENT

Watch Video 12.1 (Rothwell, 2018) where I consider the value of examinations.

Examination questions are factual to make grading easier, consistent, and more streamlined. If millions of students are taking an examination, thousands of examiners are required to grade their answers. If a question has one, and only one, right answer, you can have uniformity of grading. However, if the question allows for multiple correct answers and therefore needs to be graded qualitatively, student assessment grades will vary depending on which examiner graded whose test. This inconsistency creates a problem if we want to have a fair, unbiased, and straightforward (easy) grading system.

In life, we use the internet to find out things all the time. What would happen if we allowed children to use the internet during examinations? When I suggested

Video 12.1:
Assessment

Videos may also be accessed at **resources .corwin.com/ schoolinthecloud**.

this in a conference, a teacher said in a horrified voice, "But they will answer everything!"

I think allowing the use of the internet in an exam will change the entire system of education. Some government, somewhere, has to make a simple decision—allow the use of the internet during examinations. That one decision will change the way curricula are made, the way teachers teach, and how assessments are constructed. But will anyone do this?

This question used to trouble me a lot, but it doesn't anymore because I know it is going to happen. Technological devices are developing at such a fast rate that we will soon not be able to keep the internet out of classrooms without shutting down satellites or surgically removing implanted devices. The internet will enter the examination room, and, when it does, it will destroy the existing education system.

In the 1990s, I wrote an article called "Thinking Aloud" for the Indian magazine *Dataquest*. The article discussed a bone-conduction device that can process "soundless" speech from the bones of the jaw. In other words, the device allows others to "hear" the words you say in your head by having electrodes detect subvocalization signals. I thought this would happen by 2003, but it is happening now in 2018.

Video 12.2:
You Can Have the Entire Internet in Your Head

Videos may also be accessed at **resources .corwin.com/ schoolinthecloud**.

In 2018, researchers from the MIT Media Lab demonstrated a device that responds to soundless (subvocalized) speech, allowing users to conduct online searches without anyone knowing what they are doing (Hardesty, 2018). The device then feeds answers back into your ears. Watch Video 12.2 to see this in action.

Anyone who is using the device can be said to "know" everything, at least when it comes to "content" as opposed to "skill." In response, educators and policymakers in many countries are struggling to replace "knowing the content" models of education with inquiry-based and skills-based learning across the curriculum.

Even so, there are questions to which no one knows the answer. The internet doesn't know either. These will be the questions for the examinations of tomorrow. I imagine a world where future exams ask you to respond to questions that you will have to answer based on whatever little you can find from the internet and then interpret with your own mind.

There have always been qualitative assessments—musical instrument performance, dance, essay writing. We have methods to make such assessments. We need to use these methods for assessment in schools and state examinations. It will be expensive, but there is no choice.

Perhaps the best example of assessment where the outcomes vary from examiner to examiner is the final evaluation of a PhD thesis. The PhD is the highest degree awarded by universities. While many other degrees depend on examinations with questions that have "right" answers, the PhD examination does not. This is because a PhD is like a SOLE!

A PhD student is given a research question by her supervisor or develops one herself. No one knows the answer to the research question—after all, that is why it is a research question. The student has to figure the answer out. She has to search the unknown on her own with the guidance of her supervisor. Finally, she writes her answer in a dissertation. This has to be evaluated. At the pinnacle of our education system, we have a SOLE.

The examination for a PhD thesis is called a defense. The student presents her dissertation and her examiners (usually two) can challenge her. In some universities, such as the Indian Institute of Technology in Delhi, anyone can attend the examination and challenge her work. She then has to field the questions and defend her dissertation as best as she can. After about an hour of this, the two examiners confer together privately and come to a decision about whether she should be awarded the PhD degree or not.

Can we examine millions of school children using a method like this? Possibly yes, if each answer is graded independently by at least three examiners and their grades tested for concordance. This would work, but it would be very expensive and slow. I think a system of multiple evaluations using artificial intelligence (AI) may be the eventual way to assess children.

Some countries are thinking of removing assessments altogether. This is not really practical. If 10,000 children want to go to university, but there are only 5,000 seats, we will need a method to evaluate who will get a seat and who won't. If 200 people apply for 20 jobs, we will need a similar system.

Some countries have experimented with "portfolio" evaluation spread out over a long period of time. So instead of a single examination, a student makes a portfolio of his work over, say, a year, and that portfolio is evaluated. This is obviously a better way, but again it is expensive, subjective, and time consuming.

Some schools have experimented with peer assessment. This means each learner evaluates others. I am not sure how accurate such assessment can be, but there may be some promise. I have experimented with a method that I find interesting. It is rather similar to the jigsaw method, which John Hattie gave an effect size of 1.20 (Corwin, 2018)—equivalent to three years' learning over one year's time.

For several years, I experimented with this exercise:

A DIFFERENT TYPE OF EXAM

1) I ask a group of about 24 or so learners to each write a question about what they were learning. The question should be such that the author of the question is absolutely sure that he or she knows what to look for in the answer. In other words, the author of each question is capable of accurately grading the answers to the question that he or she has framed.

2) Once the learners submitted their questions, I removed duplicates and was usually left with about 20 questions. This became the "exam" paper.

3) I distributed the set of 20 questions to the group.

4) I asked each learner to answer all questions except the one he or she had crafted. The response to each question should be written on a separate sheet of paper indicating the learner's name and the number of the question at the top. At the end of the "exam," each learner has a completed stack of 19 sheets of paper with answers to the questions their peers crafted.

5) Assessment: Each sheet with the answer to a particular question is given to the author of that question. So the author of Question #1 receives 23 answers to his question from his peers, and so on.

6) Each learner now grades the answers, from his or her peers, to the question that learner has made.

7) When the whole process is complete, all the answer sheets are sorted by name, so that each learner's graded answers to the 19 questions are together. These are the "answer booklets."

8) Each learner then totals the grades in his or her answer booklet to calculate that learner's score.

9) Then, after sitting and doing nothing much, I collect all the scores. Without much work on my part, the examination was created, administered, and graded.

I tried this exercise for three years. Each time, the scores for each learner correlated very closely with that learner's scores on the "official" examination. However, the data are too limited to publish.

This is one of the easiest ways to assess a group of learners, if what I found is correct. You can try it. It's fun.

In *Developing Assessment-Capable Visible Learners*, Nancy Frey, John Hattie, and Douglas Fisher (2018) describe the characteristics of children who know how to learn:

- I know where I'm going.

- I have the tools for the journey.

- I monitor my own progress.

- I recognize when I'm ready for what's next.

- I know what to do next.

Such characteristics perfectly describe what I have seen in Schools in the Cloud.

Children learn about the past from their teachers and from textbooks. They learn about what happened in the world, in the arts, in the sciences, in engineering—all in the past. The system hopes that by the time they finish school, they will get a taste of everything that is known and understandable by their teachers, tucked away neatly in the folds of their brains—just in case they ever need any of it.

The future is seldom discussed.

CURRICULUM

In designing the traditional curriculum, we take everything we know and then decide what, out of that, might be relevant for schools and children, so they are "prepared" for life. The list of everything we know grows longer with time, of course, so the curriculum gets longer with time too. We try to squeeze as much as we can into the school curriculum. We remove things, but very slowly and cautiously. How do we get out of this ever-increasing curriculum?

One way might be to make a list of all the big things that we don't know yet—the "big questions of our time. Hopefully, that list will get shorter with time, unlike the list of things we do know about.

In the process of examining a big question, such as the ones we do in SOLEs, children will run into the things that we do know. For example, if we tell children about the three-body problem and how it has not been solved, they will run into what we can solve: gravitation, electromagnetic forces, and more. Maybe a curriculum of questions rather than answers will make school more interesting. In the process of investigating the big unknown, the way PhD candidates do, children would run into what we already know. When they do, they are likely to find three classes of things:

A. Things that will help them live and be useful in the future.

B. Things that they may never use but are really interesting and nice to know.

C. Things that they are never going to use, are quite boring, but are likely to be asked in an examination.

Things that fall into Class A are vital, and schools must ensure that children know them well and retain the knowledge. Things that fall into Class B are what make life worth living. Schools must make sure children are exposed to and appreciate these. Things that fall into Class C are not worth knowing, unless students are being tested on them.

A curriculum based on Class A and Class B types of knowledge will go a long way toward producing balanced problem solvers who can deal with whatever the future may throw at them.

WHERE ARE THE
SCHOOLS IN THE
CLOUD NOW?

AN UNCERTAIN FUTURE

The present status of all the projects and experiments you have read about in this book has filled me with disappointment, a sense of failure, and an awareness of my many misconceptions. These projects have also filled me with enormous hope, a sense of accomplishment, and gratitude for my many successes and for those of my colleagues. This chapter is my opportunity to reflect on all of that.

What happened to the Hole in the Wall?

It gave us a glimpse of the future of learning and of spontaneous order. Most of the original experimental sites don't exist anymore. Some still do, which is even more intriguing.

The original Hole in the Wall, the very first one in the boundary wall of NIIT, was demolished by the Delhi government to build a parking lot. When this computer in the wall was taken down, a little boy who used it, Rajinder (to me, the Neil Armstrong of self-organized learning) said, "How will I ever become an engineer?" He is now 26 and runs a tea stall near the location. He could not afford college, but when people have a problem with their phones, they come to Rajinder.

NIIT went on to create a foundation into which it incorporated the Hole in the Wall as an entity called HiWEL (Hole in the Wall Education Limited). My long-time colleague Purnendu Hota heads it. He considers me his mentor, and I hope I deserve the title. His organization continues to build Hole-in-the-Wall computers in remote or disadvantaged areas. Purnendu reports the following:

Since inception, we have installed about 1,100 Learning Stations. Each of these usually contains two user windows, i.e., 1 Learning Station = 2 user windows. We don't track children with an attendance record, so we use the following estimation to gauge how many children we are reaching:

1. *We know there is an average of 500 children in a community or school where we have the Learning Stations. This is a conservative estimate, for in some locations the number can be between 1,000 and 1,500.*

2. *We have observed that each user window caters to approximately 50 percent of the children in a year's time, so 100 percent of the children have used the Learning Station over a period of one year, i.e., approximately 500 kids in a year per Learning Station.*

3. *The usual project period is about four years, after which we give the stations over to the community or school. We can then calculate 500 children over a period of 4 years = 2000 children per station in 4 year's time (a very conservative estimate).*

4. *The overall impact, or lives touched so far, has been assessed at 1,100 Learning Stations times 2000 children = 2,200,000 children reached, i.e., about 2.2 to 2.5 million kids.*

Two and a half million children! Purnendu makes it sound so casual.

Other people are also building Hole-in-the-Wall computers. The ones I know best are called "Hello Hubs" and are built by an organization headed by my friend Katrin McMillan. The design has evolved into a high-tech kit that anyone can build, anywhere. Check out the website at Link 13.1 (hellohub.org.)

Sometimes, people ask me if I know what happened to the children who accessed the Hole-in-the-Wall computers in 1999. I did not have the means to track the thousands of children in those experiments. So I don't have an overall answer. I do have anecdotes. The best among those include the following:

- A child from the village of Shirgaon in India won a scholarship to Yale University (USA) and went on to earn a PhD in evolutionary biology.

- A child from a slum school of Hyderabad went to a Malaysian university and became a doctor.

- A little girl from Maharashtra is now a computer engineer working on a start-up.

All of them say their driving force came from the Hole in the Wall.

But feel-good stories don't establish a method, so I will stop here. Sometimes I can't help feeling that, maybe, even though I don't have statistical proof of the long-term effects of the Hole in the Wall, any one of these anecdotal cases makes it all worthwhile. You decide.

WHAT IS HAPPENING WITH THE SCHOOLS IN THE CLOUD?

Area Zero: The School in the Cloud in Gocharan has low attendance. It is now a listless, largely empty facility. Its funding ended on October 31, 2018. But Deb will become an engineer. His success will make the Gocharan project worth the time and investment.

Area One: The School in the Cloud in Korakati is in wonderful shape. It is full of children. SOLEs and the Granny Cloud have ensured rapid improvements in children's reading comprehension and internet skills. It has changed Milon's life forever. But Korakati cannot fund itself. If there is any place that needs urgent help, it is here.

Area Two: The School in the Cloud in Chandrakona is limping into normalcy, or so they say. Will someone be able to convert it into a self-sustaining business? Only time will tell in this complex place. One day, when Piya becomes a police officer, I hope she will do something about it.

Area Three: The School in the Cloud in Kalkaji does not exist anymore. But it lives on in the minds of girls like Jaya and Deepa. These girls and their friends and their children will never be maidservants. They are the successes of Kalkaji.

Areas Four, Five, and Six: The Schools in the Cloud in Phaltan, Killingworth, Newton Aycliffe, and Dasghara are working perfectly. They are an integral part of the regular schools. They actualize the future of learning and are helping create other Schools in the Cloud around the world.

I could say, dispassionately, that the seven Schools in the Cloud are like spacecraft that have completed their missions. But I am not going to say that, ever. Those spacecrafts are traveling still, some physically, some in the minds of the children who piloted them. I will take my directions from them.

SCHOOLS IN THE CLOUD SPREADING AROUND THE WORLD

Masham to Shanghai

Masham is a beautiful little market town in England, close to the town of Northallerton. There is a primary school there, almost out of a fairy tale. We did wonderful SOLEs there for several years with two classes, Year 4 students and Year 6 students, who had a teacher with a lovely sense of humor Two teachers and the principal of the school came to India for the Granny Cloud conference. They went to Korakati on a boneshaker van and were never the same again (in a good way).

One of the teachers was a great champion of SOLEs, and I hope she still is.

I told her about the experiments with trying GCSE A-Level questions with Year 4 and Year 6 students in the SOLE mode. The two teachers tried it and got the same results. They began to talk about it wherever they went. One of the teachers, in particular, attributed her change of attitude to her involvement with SOLEs.

In 2017, one of the teachers got an offer from an international school in Shanghai. She moved to Shanghai, and one of the first things she did was to invite me to her school. I was in Calcutta at the time, and it was an easy trip. I did a few SOLEs there. In less than a year, she was promoted to assistant principal and was given a grant to set up School in the Cloud facilities in three of her schools. I inaugurated them!

As for me, I feel a bit like Chanakya (the *Kauṭilya*). Look that up if you need to.

Figure 13.1 Suzhou, China: A Perfectly Implemented School in the Cloud

Goa, India

India has always been a challenge when it comes to SOLEs. The Indian education system is purely Victorian, stuck in the nineteenth century. It is driven by discipline, memorization, and a grim, unsmiling outlook.

So it was with a great deal of excitement that I read this email in November of 2015.

November 2015

Dear Sugata

Many thanks for all your brilliant work—I have been exploring and enjoying :)
  I set up a primary school in South Goa last year and am now poised to open a secondary school in North Goa in Sept 2016.
  I am proposing for it to be a "Google Green School," i.e., driven by the two most important forces that will shape the next generation—technology and the environment. I intend it to be a showcase of what is possible: how the internet and computers can positively move forward the paradigm of education and update it from its current lack of imagination or true purpose.
  I would love for it to be part of your SOLE experiment—we can set our school up in exactly that way from Day 1.
  Obviously, I have some concerns about how to reconcile these ideas with the needs of parents, mainly, e.g., their children passing exams, but I am looking into "non-traditional pathways" into university and higher education—they do exist. . . . .

All the best,
Shilpa Mehta

Shilpa turned out to be an extremely capable woman. Within months, she had rented a huge Portuguese villa in Goa and set up her school.

I went to visit Paradise School, Goa, in 2016 and was amazed by what she had achieved.

The school was driven by the idea of SOLEs, and I did the very first SOLE there on the day she inaugurated it. The question was "How does a mobile phone know where it is?" The usual buzz of the SOLE followed, and then we heard words that aren't usually spoken by 12-year-old voices: "satellites," "triangles," "Why does three keep popping up?" and so on. I was waiting for one word, and it came about 30 minutes into the SOLE—"Trigonometry," said a voice. I knew spontaneous order had appeared.

Shilpa brought SOLEs into mainstream Indian schooling. Her school is fast becoming one of the biggest and most appreciated in Goa.

The Isle of Man, United Kingdom

Helen Moyer is a teacher in a lovely school on the Isle of Man. It is called Willaston and is headed by a very efficient principal, Rose Burton.

> *Good morning*
>   *I am currently reading your book* Beyond the Hole in the Wall. *I was wondering if you could advise me if there are any training sessions in the near future?*
>   *Also, I am very keen to observe further SOLEs for both children and adults and would be delighted if you could recommend some places to visit.*
>
> *Thank you for your time.*
> *Kind regards*
> *Helen Moyer*

At the first opportunity, I took a plane to the Isle of Man. What followed were several SOLEs in Willaston. In one of them, I tried a question that was different from our usual questions: it was not about a subject.

"Suppose you are 9 years old and live in Dubai with a 65-year-old aunt. Your father, who is away for a year, has sent you £200 to take your aunt for a weekend holiday. What's the best holiday you could do?"

The humming and buzzing of the SOLE became deafening as the children rushed about, looking at what each group was doing and then vehemently disagreeing with it.

"Do you have any idea how much a Coke costs in a hotel?"

"How many steps can she climb before falling down? She is 65!"

That sort of thing.

It was a question that would lead them into accounts, advertising, online booking, internet spam marketing, health, foreign exchange, and a host of areas that are, well, somewhere in the curriculum, I suppose.

After about 40 minutes, two stunning answers appeared.

First, a group of boys had worked out a way to purchase a holiday for two days for two people, including airfare from Dubai to Manchester! They showed us, meticulously, how it is possible.

The second answer was from a group of three girls. They said they did not want to waste their meager funds on travel time. "We are not rich," they said. "We can't ever afford to see what it's like inside a really big hotel." So their holiday would be two nights at a discounted rate at the seven-star Burj Al Arab Jumeirah in Dubai.

SOLEs are about questions to which there may not be a single unambiguous answer. That's the way it is in life, is it not?

There were observers from the government watching the SOLE, and I was invited to conduct a training session on SOLEs for all the teachers of the island. The Isle of Man has its own government and can make independent decisions about education. I accepted nervously, and when it happened a few months later, it was an exhilarating experience.

Helen Moyer was taken off teaching duty and put in charge of the island-wide implementation of SOLEs.

If anyone can do it, she can.

Harlem, New York, United States

Natalia Vega was one of our newest Grannies in the Granny Cloud in 2013. Originally from Colombia and settled in New York, she worked with poor Black and Hispanic children in Harlem, New York. She was a brilliant Granny, with a natural talent for SOLEs with children. In July 2013, she enrolled at Newcastle University as one of my PhD students. She completed the PhD in just four years and was ready for the degree in 2018, which she received after she submitted some minor corrections to her dissertation.

I managed to provide Natalia with some funding from my lecture fees, and she built a School in the Cloud in her school in Harlem, called John B. Russwurm P.S. 197M. She spent less than $5,000. We were getting close to an inexpensive design. I was there for the inauguration on October 14, 2015.

I asked the children to make a question. "Why do dogs chase cats?" they asked. To my amazement, the children started to investigate violence. Dogs do not want to be violent, but the cats think they do. The cats unsheathe their claws; the dogs misunderstand. What followed was a description of the violence that can come from misunderstood intentions.

Ohio, United States

In 2014, Dr. Jeffrey McLellan launched an initiative to bring SOLEs to the United States and beyond. He started with an app called STARTSOLE. Jeff started with the premise that facilitating teachers to conduct SOLEs without training is key to the spread of SOLEs. I had not thought of this. When I asked Jeff what has happened since, he wrote the following, in a very matter of fact way:

> Four years later, the results from the launch of this tool and its adoption among educators has been impressive. We have evidence that The STARTSOLE™ process was designed to facilitate an educator's ability to seamlessly apply inquiry learning with as little pretraining or cost to the educator or school as possible. Over the period 2014–2018, STARTSOLE has established an installed base of over 10,000 educators (predominantly K–12) living in 90 countries. These educators work in over 2,500 schools, and the STARTSOLE™ experience has reached an estimated 400,000 K–12 students. As part of the pilot launch of STARTSOLE™, a data collection system was integrated into the delivery and use of the mobile application. STARTSOLE™ has the potential to bring student-centered inquiry learning into every classroom and into the hands of every educator.

He wants to reach 10 million students in the United States by 2021.
I want to buy him lunch.

Larissa, Greece

Larissa is the largest and capital city of the Thessaly region of Greece. It is the region where Achilles, the warrior, was born and lived (remember the vulnerability of the Achilles' heel?). Larissa is mentioned by Homer in the Iliad. It is also the city where the father of western medicine, Hippocrates, practiced and died.

Vasiliki Mandalou is a philosophy and language teacher who lives in Larissa. I met her at a conference in Istanbul and later went to Larissa for another conference. Vasiliki took me to a little private school to conduct a SOLE. The children were reasonably good at English, and I decided to do a SOLE about communication. These children were between 12 and 15 years old.

I asked them, "Sometimes, when we say something to a person, that person understands something else, right?" They nodded, and we discussed why people might misunderstand each other. I drew a simple house on the whiteboard, just a square with a triangular roof. Then I erased it.

"Do you remember what I drew?" I asked. The children nodded.

"Well, suppose I am a computer, and you can ask me to draw. What would you ask to get that picture back?"

"Draw a house," said a child.

"I don't know what a house is," I said.

"Draw a square."

I drew a huge square covering the whole whiteboard.

"No no, draw a small square," they laughed.

I drew a tiny square in one corner of the whiteboard.

After a moment of quiet, a child spoke.

"Draw a square with sides of 20 centimeters at the center of the board."

I did what he said.

"Now draw a triangle on top of the square"

I drew a huge upside-down triangle, with its point down, on top of the square. More laughter.

Finally, after a lot of frustration and laughter, they got it.

"Draw a square with sides of 20 centimeters at the center of the board. Then, starting with the top left corner of the square, draw a triangle whose tip is about 10 centimeters over the center of the top side of the square."

I said it might be even easier if they labeled the corners of the square A, B, C, and D. In about half an hour, they started commanding me with the language of geometry.

I told them this was a new language from their country. Created by a man called Euclid, a very long time ago.

This language was very hard to misunderstand.

"But where did language come from in the first place? Do animals have language?"

A SOLE followed.

The children told us about the origins of language from animal sounds and exclamations. That's why "cough" sounds like a cough. They spoke of how words might have formed and how words can have different meanings, leading to misunderstanding. I think Euclid would have been happy.

As I left the SOLE, a boy came up to me.

"Are you a teacher in training?" he asked.

"Well, sort of," I said.

"You should carry on," he said. "You will make a very good teacher."

"Thank you," I said proudly that day in the city of Achilles and Hippocrates.

Punjab, India

In the summer of 2016, Ritu and Natalia were hired by a tech start-up in California to build two tiny Schools in the Cloud in remote villages in Mohali, a suburb of Chandigarh, the capital of Punjab. I offered to help manage the project remotely—for free.

Natalia chose a village called Aloona Tola. Ritu chose one called Sidhuwal. Both were about an hour's drive from Mohali. I got them to build the two facilities quickly and not make a fuss about it. They got the SinCs up in January 2018, in less than a month, and started measuring reading comprehension every 10 days or so. By then, the data from the TED project Schools in the Cloud had come in, so I knew what I was doing.

Natalia's data, as given in Figure 13.2, shows a linear increase in reading comprehension. This increase is similar to that shown by Suneeta's data for a similar year-group in Phaltan (Figure 7.6). And, Ritu's data (Figure 11.3) showed the same nonlinear shape as Suneeta's data for very young children (Figure 7.2).

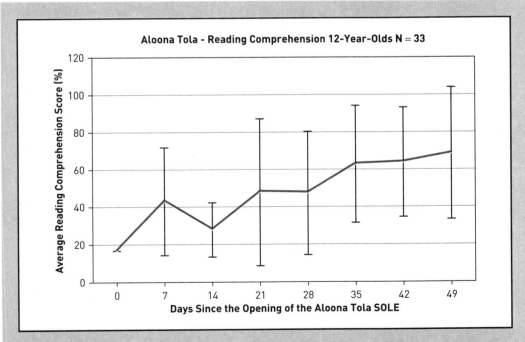

Figure 13.2 Aloona Tola: Growth in Reading Comprehension, February 2018

It is from Suneeta, Ritu, and Natalia's data and qualitative observations that I learned not to trust "fluency." I saw examples from everywhere of children who could read a passage fluently and rapidly—without understanding a word of what the content was.

I did not have to wait for Ritu and Natalia's data to get analyzed. Two months into the project, officials from the Punjab government came to find out how the children of these remote places were reading and speaking in English. Actually, the children were reading and speaking just a few words in an incomprehensible accent, but the locals still could not believe what was happening. There was no teacher, you see.

A few weeks later, Ritu wrote to inform me that the Punjab government had decided to create Schools in the Cloud in 56 government primary schools in the state. Here was impact at a scale I had not seen anywhere. It turned out later that the deputy commissioner was quite aware of my work, as was the commissioner himself. It's just that they did not think the results of SOLEs would be so visible in such a short time.

Ritu helped create the 56 Schools in the Cloud, and they became operational in November 2018. The deputy commissioner now has funds for 25 more. This is the largest government effort with SOLEs in the world.

Bristol, England

James Stanfield, my long-term colleague at Newcastle University and the anchor of our research center, SOLE Central, received an email from out of the blue. It was from a teacher, Sarah Thomas, in a school called St. Barnabas in Bristol.

Dear SOLE Central,

I am a teacher and English lead in a primary school at St. Barnabas School in South Gloucestershire, Bristol, and felt I should contact you to share what we are doing in our school and the success we have seen.

I have very much admired the work by Sugata Mitra for a while, and this year I was given free rein to introduce "School in the Cloud" into our curriculum (we call it SOLE Time). I introduced "SOLE Time" into the school's guided reading policy, which means each week every child from Year 2 through 6 has half an hour to use SOLE skills to research an open-ended question. The students then present to the rest of the class. It has been a massive success and has completely transformed our school for the better. It has also completely transformed the children's attitudes to learning, work ethic, and skills.

Last term (May 11), we had a visit from Ofsted, and SOLE Time was mentioned in our report:

As confident young learners, pupils are ambitious for themselves and supportive of each other. Pupils really enjoy their time in the special research room, which you and your team have developed. The SOLE (Self Organised Learning Environment) project is a good example of your drive to go beyond usual classroom learning in order to provide pupils with opportunities to develop their own learning habits and to think for themselves.

It has been such a success that we are now going to base our topic curriculum around "School in the Cloud" and complete a project-based learning approach. We are only able to do this due to the skills children have picked up during SOLE Time. I have also been asked by my local authority learning advisors to support other schools with their reading action plan and share the School in the Cloud approach.

A link to this school's Ofsted report can be found on our companion website (Link 13.2).

Here was our second reference by Ofsted. I wrote to Sarah and subsequently visited her school. I did a SOLE with the children, and then Sarah did another one.

She is way better at it than I am.

That day, in Bristol, I felt a wave of relief sweep over me.

I must end this chapter with one last story—possibly the most prophetic of the lot.

On December 12, 2016, I visited West Thornton Primary Academy in Croydon, England. Teachers and staff wanted to discuss SOLEs with me and show me around their school, which was a remarkably imaginative feat of design. I conducted a SOLE, and the children wanted to chat some more.

"What do you think of learning from the internet?" I asked. "Is it just looking up stuff and copying it down?"

The children shook their heads vehemently.

"So what is different then?" I asked.

A boy of about 12 stood up and spoke.

"On the internet, you know before you learn," he said.

He showed me the future of learning.

PROJECTION, PREDICTION, PROPHECY, AND PHANTASY

LOOKING FOR THE FUTURE

The Hole-in-the-Wall experiments, like a weathervane, had pointed at a new future for learning, one that I ignored at the time. It took 20 years for me to figure out that the Hole in the Wall was pointing at the School in the Cloud.

And now, the School in the Cloud is pointing at the future again. This time I am not going to ignore it. What the weathervane is pointing at now is blurred by time, but I am going to peer through the mist, if I can.

Should a book like this look at the future at all? So far, this book has been about experiments with learning, and the outcomes have shown what schools can do differently to enable children to learn what is relevant to them today. I could have just left it there, as a manual for creating and using Schools in the Cloud. But that is not good enough anymore. We are on a technological trajectory for human development that is now in its exponential phase. The future is arriving faster than ever before. If we don't try to guess at where the School in the Cloud will go, this book will not be fit for its time. We have to take a look at the future, no matter how strange, how esoteric, and how alien it may be. Then, we have to prepare to take our schools there.

Between the time I began writing this book, in late 2017, and now, in early 2019, the internet has already changed much of traditional teaching into the least efficient and most expensive way to learn anything. "Groups of children can learn anything from the internet," I had written in 2008, after the Kalikuppam experiment. At that time, it was considered a naïve and extreme point of view. From Korakati to Killingworth, the children of the School in the Cloud have shown us otherwise.

We have to look into the future, as far as we can.

At the turn of the last century, I was asked to write about the future, and I wrote an article called "Eight Powers of Ten" (Mitra, 2001), imagining the years from 2000 to the year 10,002,000. While writing this article, I realized that there are a few things one can do to find possible futures. It's not just guesswork, or, at least, it need not be. I think we use four different ways to see the future—projection, prediction, prophecy, and phantasy.

PROJECTION

You can start with a very basic assumption. The future will be at least as different from the present as the present is from the past. For example, 2028 will be at least as different from 2018 as 2018 is from 2010. In 2010, few thought that one day cars would be able to drive themselves. In 2018, everyone thought so. So we might project that, in 2028, few will know that there was a time when cars were driven by people. This is a simple and possibly quite accurate view of the future. This is a linear projection and works well over short periods of time.

As long as the changes from the past to the future are happening at a constant rate, your prediction will work. You are driving steadily on a highway. During the last minute, your car went 2 kilometers; in the next minute, it will go another 2 kilometers. Easy and accurate. In this book, we have seen many instances when children's internet searching skills increased at a linear rate in Schools in the Cloud.

If you are in the middle of a school year, you can safely predict their searching skill levels at the end of the year.

But, projection has its limitations. When you are crossing a road at a place where there are no pedestrian crossing lights, you look at a car coming toward you, estimate how long it will take to reach you, and then cross or stay where you are. You would assume that the car is traveling at a constant speed. If the car were accelerating, your prediction would fail, and you would either have to scream and run as fast as you can or, unfortunately, get hit. Also, projection does not work over long periods of time because things usually don't change at a constant rate over long periods of time. You can't guess how tall your child will be at age 21 by looking at how tall she was at ages 10, 11, and 12.

You can predict 2028 from 2018 by examining 2010, but you can't predict 2118 from 2018 by examining 1918. Most things change nonlinearly over the centuries. You need another way of looking into the future.

PREDICTION

There are many ways in which things can change over time. If you can measure the change, you can make a graph of it and use this to make predictions. Even if you can't measure something easily, for example, how happy you are feeling, you can still make a mental graph of what will happen to your happiness. In Figure 14.1, I have tried to show some kinds of graphs you could create, when going from the past to the future.

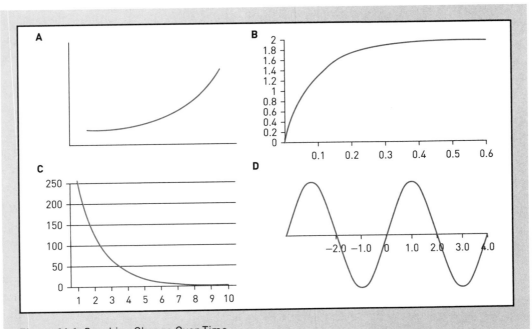

Figure 14.1 Graphing Change Over Time

Let's take a closer look. Graph A depicts something that increases slowly to start with but speeds up as it goes along. We have seen something like that in the reading comprehension curve at Sidhuwal.

Graph B depicts an increase that happens rapidly but then stops happening. It could graph your child's height, for example. Rapid improvement often makes us very optimistic, only to create disappointment when the improvement slows down and stops. But a rapid growth in some negative change, say, for example, cancer or global warming, can create fear initially and then, perhaps, guarded optimism.

Graph C shows a rapid decrease until there is no more room for a decrease, as the charted change hits rock bottom. This is like when you are losing weight on a wonderful diet, and then, gradually, the weight loss stops, except that, of course, the data would even out well before the zero shown in the graph! Most often, sadly, the "rock bottom" of weight loss occurs even before a dieter reaches optimum weight. If you knew the curve in advance, maybe you would feel a bit less sorry for yourself.

Graph D shows a wave. Here things go up and down, again and again. But perhaps we should say things increase and decrease, as the chart could mark an increase and decrease of either human health or human mortality. This wave-like change is common in human history— empires rise and fall, only to see another rise again. So do our joys and miseries. Whatever goes up comes down.

No, I got that last example wrong. Whatever goes up does come down on this Earth of ours. But—as we all, tragically, know—whatever comes down often never goes up again. Physicists hide this under an abstruse word, "entropy." Nature goes from order to disorder, they say. But they may not be entirely right.

So when you want to predict the future, if you know the curve of the trend, or if you can guess at it, you could make really great predictions. The kind that people will marvel at! Some gamblers can do this very well. And we, teachers, are we not the greatest gamblers of them all?

With good predictive ability, you can get to see the future tens and hundreds of years away, perhaps thousands—but not much more. So is that the limit as to how far into the future we can see?

Fortunately, there is a way to see further.

PROPHECY

So far, we have seen that projection and prediction can provide us with fairly accurate views of the future, but only to the extent to which the trends apply. However, throughout human history, there have been people who have said that they can see into the distant future. They were prophets. When asked how, they usually referred to an unidentifiable source that "spoke" to them.

Recently, in 2018, there were severe floods in the state of Kerala in India. Many people died, and many had to leave their homes. Indian TV recorded an interview with an 8-year-old girl who had urged her family to move to the top of a neighboring tall building. She carried a container full of cotton soaked in lime water. When asked why she did this, she said the main water supply could not rise to the height of the building, so the upper floors where full of smoke. The lime water would absorb carbon dioxide from the many fires in the region. When asked if she had learned this from her teachers in school, she said, "No, external," and was silent. I think she meant the internet but was too scared to mention that because accessing the internet is not allowed in school. I don't think she even remembered when and where she had read this. The voice in her head was from the network. Her action was a prophecy.

Can prophecy have an understandable basis?

I turn to Skinner and Einstein, who said similar things about education.

"Education is what survives when what has been learned has been forgotten," wrote Skinner (1964).

What does "forgotten" mean? Is it the erasure of the neural connections that make up memory, or is it the submergence of these interconnections into the inaccessible subconscious?

Is "what survives" the voice from the submerged neural network that prophets describe?

Maybe prophecy is prediction, using trends that are inaccessible to our conscious minds. Or maybe it's our hidden desires, surfacing as messages. Maybe prophecy is just wishful thinking.

Whatever its nature may be, prophecies are real. They can span eons and have driven human reality for millennia. Maybe, we can learn to prophesy. We don't know how as yet.

Even prophecy, though, does not cross the boundaries of reality as we perceive it. It still talks of humans and earth, space and time.

Can we not see any further than that?

PHANTASY

As Sigmund Freud (1917/1976) wrote, humans "cannot subsist on the scanty satisfaction which they can extort from reality. 'We simply cannot do without auxiliary constructions,' as Theodor Fontane once said . . . [without] dwelling on imaginary wish-fulfillments."

I did not use the common spelling "fantasy" to describe this final process of seeing the future. This is because the old spelling "phantasy" starts with a "p" and goes nicely with projection, prediction, and prophecy. Second, because I read a strangely attractive idea that fantasy, when it resides in the subconscious or the unconscious mind is called phantasy!

Phantasy is outside of our consciousness, outside of our reality. It can take us anywhere. If we did not need this ability, we would not have it. Phantasy depends on imagination, and we don't know much about what that means. *Wikipedia* defines imagination as follows:

> **Imagination** is the ability to produce and simulate novel objects, peoples and ideas in the mind without any immediate input of the senses. It is also described as the forming of experiences in the mind, which can be re-creations of past experiences, such as vivid memories with imagined changes, or . . . completely invented. . . . Imagination helps make knowledge applicable in solving problems and is fundamental to integrating experience and the learning process. (Imagination, 2019)

If imagination works without the input of the senses, then it must emerge from the neural network of our brains. Imagination defies entropy; it produces spontaneous order out of chaos.

SPONTANEOUS ORDER

A network is created by connecting things together. Each connected thing is called a "node" of the network. When something happens to a node, the other nodes connected to it are also affected. Since these affected nodes are connected to other nodes, eventually, all the nodes in the system are affected by what happened to the first affected node. But it doesn't stop there.

All the affected nodes eventually affect the node that started it all. That node reacts, and the process starts all over again. This network is called a "complex dynamical system," as we discussed in the prelude to this book.

There is a simple experiment that illustrates this phenomenon. It is very easy to do, and I have done it many times. You can try this with any group of people. Ask the group to clap in unison, in step. That's all. Don't make any gestures to illustrate what you mean.

Now carefully listen to what happens. You will hear a first second or two of random claps—then the claps will come together as though a conductor were directing them.

Who brought those claps together? Who decided the frequency? Who decided the volume?

Well, no one did. It just happened. Spontaneous order appears by itself.

When all the people start clapping, each clap of each person is heard by all the others. This alters the clapping of all the other listeners; they clap differently. The difference makes all the clappers clap differently.

One affects the many, and the many affect the one—until spontaneous order appears.

Try this with children, say 12-year-olds. Then set up a SOLE with the question, "How did the claps come together?" Tell them no one knows the answer.

The fact that complex dynamical systems produce spontaneous order has been known for a long time. This is the basis for life itself. All our joys and sorrows, all our achievements and perversions are the results of spontaneous order. Our reality—clapping in unison.

Here is another question you could ask anyone: "Does the internet exist?" People will look strangely at you. Then ask, "Where is it?" Enjoy the silence.

In the School in the Cloud, your children should learn to expand the span of their past and their view of the future. Then they must use these to construct their actions and plans. Their assessments must look for the span of their perception of time.

Children need to practice imagining. We do too little of that in school. That's all I am trying to say.

In order to prepare children to take the right actions in life, they need knowledge of the past that they can use, and they need the ability to imagine a future. Then they need to combine the two inputs—from the past and the future—and choose an action. Then they will write their own reality.

This is education.

EPILOGUE

At MIT, I had begun to work on expanding an idea about what consciousness might be. Nicholas Negroponte warned me, "There are people like Marvin Minsky and Noam Chomsky working on this. Why don't you lay off and stick to self-organized learning?" I argued with him endlessly and was often rude—something that I am terribly ashamed about. I apologize to Nicholas on these pages.

Nevertheless. . . .

Spontaneous order appearing from interacting "many-body" systems is how nature works. It has been in operation from the birth of the universe, when the chaotic interaction of particles formed the stars, planets, and galaxies, to the beginning of life on our planet, when the chaotic interaction of carbon and hydrogen (and later other atoms) formed the amino acids and sugars that would order themselves into the RNA molecule and then DNA. The immense effort of this one molecule, DNA, to survive through evolution created life, first in water and then on land—leading to the emergence of *Homo sapiens*.

Spontaneous order in a global network of people characterizes this time in human history. The internet exists yet has no physical form. It is not material. It thinks and is probably conscious, but we may never be able to understand, or even sense, this alien consciousness—any more than an individual neuron can sense the thoughts and consciousness of a brain.

Humans build machines. In a few thousand years, these machines have progressed from simple tools to complex, interacting silicon structures that can sense their world, and think. Artificial intelligence was first proposed in the 1950s by people such as Alan Turing, John McCarthy, and Marvin Minsky, but it had to wait for almost 50 years for computing capability to improve to a point where artificial neural networks and the resultant emergent phenomenon (spontaneous order) were practical and usable. These devices are now everywhere, and we live with them. They learn continuously, improving their sense of the past and having a limited, linear ability to see the future. They can project and predict but have no imagination or any capability for prophecy or phantasy. Yet.

These silicon brains will get integrated into our biological structures. A composite creature is imminent. It would "know" everything—before it learns. Humans will be the first species on Earth to affect its own evolution directly. As the new species emerges, the already crumbling education systems of our time will have to evolve to another system. Extending and enriching the effect of our past and improving our ability to see the future through projection, prediction, prophecy, and phantasy will become the only goal of this evolved educational system. This is what the schools of today have to evolve into. And then. . . .

The carbon-silicon composite creature will shrink to quantum dimensions and finally lose all its material form. Is there life other than us?—the burning question of the twenty-first century—will turn out to be a mistake of phraseology. Our kind of life is a primitive exception. Anything that can connect to form non-material networks is conscious, and alive. We were looking for the wrong thing, while surrounded by consciousness.

Consciousness, too, evolves. As it loses its connections with space, it is left to evolve only in time. Its actions are affected by all of the past, from the beginning of time. And its actions are affected by all of the future, to the end of time. It will evolve, someday, to reach its final ability.

To read reality—before it is written.

THE SCHOOL IN THE CLOUD
DOCUMENTARY DISCUSSION GUIDE

Thank you for viewing *The School in the Cloud*! We hope that you enjoyed the film and that it prompts you to reflect on the future of learning in your own classroom and school. We have provided the following discussion guide to aid in your reflection. We recommend that you answer the questions in conversation with colleagues, parents, administrators, and, of course, with students. The documentary *The School in the Cloud* is available for purchase at https://new.tugg.com/titles/the-school-in-the-cloud.

SELF-ORGANIZED LEARNING

1. How does technology change education? How should technology impact our assessment system?

If school were to be about the biggest questions that humankind faces today, if school were to be about what we don't know, rather than long lists of what we do know, the School in the Cloud would be a major and vital resource for children.

2. Is the internet a threat or a catalyst to learning?

In his 2020 book, *The School in the Cloud*, Sugata Mitra writes about conducting Self-Organized Learning Environments (SOLEs) for the first time in Buenos Aires, Argentina:

It was here that I conducted the first SOLE sessions in Spanish. Mabel Quiroga translated and the children and I had a whale of a time. It is here that I discovered that a SOLE would work in any language, provided there were enough online resources in that language.

3. What role can SOLEs play in English language acquisition? Do you think children could learn any language through SOLEs? Why or why not?

4. What impact can learning from technology have not only on children's achievement scores, but on their aspirations?

5. Why is it important that the children learn in groups? How do the members of a group help guide the SOLE?

6. In the film, Sugata Mitra says, "I'm willing to take a bet that the evil influences of the internet, which will of course be there, will be considerably less than the good it does." What are the risks of allowing children to search freely online? Do you agree that the potential benefits are worth the risks?

We found that if children work on large, publicly visible screens, there is not much need for any filter or other policing mechanisms to prevent "misuse" (usually a euphemism for accses to internet pornography or other undesirable images). Groups of heterogeneous children, i.e. boys and girls together, working in a public space where any passersby can see what they are doing, tend to focus on things that will not get them into trouble.

MINIMALLY INVASIVE EDUCATION

7. Sugata Mitra reports that children's scores in India raised from 30% to 50% after the introduction of a friendly mediator, who admired the children using the "method of the grandmother." Why do you think the Granny Cloud was so effective?

8. What is a teacher's role in Schools in the Cloud? How do you think the role of teachers will change as the internet is incorporated into more schools?

9. The documentary reports the critical importance of designing "big questions" to drive students' curiosity and inquiry online. How do you craft these big questions?

Children who are used to doing SOLE sessions will not need much instruction or encouragement. They generally love it—if you do it right.

THE ROLE OF RESEARCH

A long time ago, it was a problem to carry coal up to the top of a mine in a colliery. George Stephenson solved the problem by improving upon the steam engines and the locomotives already in use at the collieries of his day. Stephenson's machine was huge and sat on top of the colliery, pulling a rope tied to wagons of coal that moved up a track. Then he made the engine small enough to mount on to one of the wagons so that the whole thing, engine and all, could move along the track. No one understood how it worked, but the coal went up the slope to where it had to go. When he first demonstrated it, people said, 'It will never start.' Then, when his engine, the Rocket as it was called, started to roll, they said, 'It will never stop.' Scientists began to frantically search for how the steam engine worked. A new branch of physics called thermodynamics was discovered and went on to change our view of the entire universe!

Stephenson solved the problem first; the research came later.

10. How much research is necessary before a teaching or learning strategy should be tried and implemented?

11. How do you approach implementing a new strategy in your classroom/school? What success indicators do you look for?

12. What do the competing narratives about the Hole in the Wall (that of its success as a "sign" of the future of learning, and that of its failure to be sustainable) show about the nature of research in education? Do you side with either perspective?

SCHOOLS IN THE CLOUD

13. The documentary shows Schools in the Cloud in both India and the United Kingdom. What factors do you think contributed to their success in each location? Could Schools in the Cloud work anywhere in the world?

14. Consider the story of Priya, the young girl who attends the School in the Cloud in Chandrakona. What difference could the School in the Cloud make in her life?

15. What do you think will happen to Schools in the Cloud in the future?

16. The documentary shows that the School in the Cloud in Korakati encounters many problems with acquiring reliable internet access—and as a result, learning stalls in Korakati. Why do you think that is? What is responsible for the turnaround in Korakati, when it "comes back to life"?

17. What will it take for Schools in the Cloud in remote areas such as Korakati to succeed?

The School in the Cloud in Korakati is in wonderful shape. It is full of children. SOLEs and the Granny Cloud have ensured rapid improvements in children's reading comprehension and internet skills. [...] But Korakati cannot fund itself. If there is any place that needs urgent help, it is here.

18. The documentary shows teacher Amy-Leigh Douglas at George Stephenson High School asking her students, "If you had to design a room for learning, what would you want?" If you could design your own space for learning, what would it look like? How would it feel for you and your students?

19. Are you considering starting your own School in the Cloud? If so, what have you learned from the documentary to guide in building and running your own?

20. At the end of the documentary, Sugata Mitra says, "That's the best thing that a research project can do . . . not so much produce the answers as produce the next set of questions." What further questions does the School in the Cloud raise for you? What are your next steps in finding the answers?

REFERENCES

Arora, P. (2010). Hope-in-the-wall? A promise of free learning. *British Journal of Educational Technology, 41*(5), 689–702. Retrieved from https://doi.org/10.1111/j .1467-8535.2010.01078.x

Banerjee, A., & Duflo, E. (2011, September 10). Pratham's contributions to Indian education policy debate [Excerpt from *Poor economies*]. *TechSangam*. Retrieved from http://www.tech sangam.com/2011/09/10/prathams-contributions-to-indian-education-policy-debate/

Birkegaard, A., Oxenhandler, D., & Sloan, W. (2018). *The open window* [Documentary film]. Denmark: Videnskabsstudier, Roskilde University.

Clark, D. (2013, March 4). Sugata Mitra: Slum chic? 7 reasons for doubt. *Donald Clark Plan B* [Blog]. Retrieved from http://donaldclarkplanb.blogspot.com/search?q=mitra

Corwin. (2018, October). *Visible Learning*plus—*250+ influences on student achievement.* Thousand Oaks, CA: Corwin. Retrieved from https://us.corwin.com/sites/default/ files/250_influences_10.1.2018.pdf

Freud, S. (1976). Lecture 23: The paths to the formation of symptoms. In James Strachey & A. Richards (Eds.), *Introductory lectures on psychoanalysis* (pp. 404–424). London: Penguin, p. 419. Original work published in 1917.

Frey, N., Hattie, J., & Fisher, D. (2018). *Developing assessment-capable visible learners, Grades K–12: Maximizing skill, will, and thrill.* Thousand Oaks, CA: Corwin.

Grove, J. (2016). I don't need to know everything; I just need to know where to find it when I need it. *S.O.L.E.* [Website section]. Retrieved from the Belleville Primary School web- site at https://www.belleville-school.org.uk/news/s-o-l-e

Hardesty, L. (2018, April 4). Computer system transcribes words users "speak silently": Electrodes on the face and jaw pick up otherwise undetectable neuromuscular sig- nals triggered by internal verbalizations. *MIT News*. Retrieved from http://news.mit .edu/2018/computer-system-transcribes-words-users-speak-silently-0404

Hattie, J. A. (2009). *Visible learning: A synthesis of over 800 meta-analyses relating to achievement.* New York, NY: Routledge.

Hattie, J. A. (2012). *Visible learning for teachers: Maximizing impact on learning.* New York, NY: Routledge.

Hattie, J. A., & Donoghue, G. M. (2016). Learning strategies: A synthesis and conceptual model. *npj Science of Learning, 1,* 16013.

Imagination. (2019, May 29). *Wikipedia*. Retrieved from https://en.wikipedia.org/wiki/ Imagination

Jenkins, L. (2008). *From systems thinking to systemic action: 48 key questions to guide the journey.* Lanham, MD: Rowen & Littlefield Education.

Klein, N. (1918). Address of Nicholas Klein. In *Documentary history of the Amalgamated Clothing Workers of America, 1916–1918* (pp. 51–53). Baltimore: Amalgamated Clothing Workers of America.

Kulkarni, S., & Mitra, S. (2010). The use of self-organizing systems of learning for improving the quality of schooling for children in remote areas. Project Report. Newcastle University.

Leonard, S. (2016, November 9). Urging students to teach themselves. *Positive News.* Retrieved from https://www.positive.news/perspective/urging-students-to -teach-themselves/

Mancuso, S. (2010). *The roots of plant intelligence.* Retrieved from https://www.ted.com/talks/stefano_mancuso_the_roots_of_plant_intelligence

McDonald, A. S. (2001). The prevalence and effects of test anxiety in school children. *Educational Psychology, 21*(1), 89–101. https://www.tandfonline.com/doi/abs/10.1080/01443410020019867

Mitra, S. (2001). Eight powers of ten. *Barefoot in the head* [Blog]. Original article reposted December 30, 2015, and available from http://sugatam.blogspot.com/2015/12/in-2001-i -was-asked-to-write-article.html

Mitra, S. (2009). Remote presence: Technologies for "beaming" teachers where they cannot go. *Journal of Emerging Technologies in Web Intelligence, 1*(1), 55–59. Retrieved from https://media-openideo-rwd.oiengine.com/attachments/318b8cc44849fd5ab9606 0be3d0597c54354263f.pdf

Mitra, S. (2012). *Beyond the Hole in the Wall: Discover the power of self-organized learning.* New York and Vancouver: TED Conferences, LLC.

Mitra, S., & Crawley, E. (2014). Effectiveness of self-organised learning by children: Gateshead experiments. *Journal of Education and Human Development, 3*(3), 79–88. Retrieved from http://jehdnet.com/journals/jehd/Vol_3_No_3_September_2014/6.pdf

Mitra, S., & Dangwal, R. (2010). Limits to self-organising systems of learning—the Kalikuppam experiment. *British Journal of Educational Technology, 41*(5), 672–688. Retrieved from https://onlinelibrary.wiley.com/doi/abs/10.1111/j.1467-8535.2010.01077.x

Mitra, S., & Dangwal, R. (2017). Acquisition of computer literacy skills through self-organizing systems of learning among children in Bhutan and India. *Prospects 47*(3), 275–292. Retrieved from https://link.springer.com/article/10.1007/s11125-017-9409 -6?wt_mc=Internal.Event.1.SEM.ArticleAuthorOnlineFirst

Mitra, S., Dangwal, R., Chatterjee, S., Jha, S., Bisht, R. S., & Kapur, P. (2005). Acquisition of computer literacy on shared public computers: Children and the "Hole in the Wall." *Australasian Journal of Educational Technology, 21*(3), 407–426. Retrieved from https://ajet.org.au/index.php/AJET/article/view/1328

Mitra, S., Dangwal, R., & Thadani, L. (2008). Effects of remoteness on the quality of education: A case study from North Indian Schools. *Australasian Journal of Educational Technology, 24*(2), 168–180. Retrieved from https://ajet.org.au/index.php/AJET/article/view/1219

Mitra, S., & Kumar, S. (2006). Fractal replication in time-manipulated one-dimensional cellular automata. *Complex Systems, 16*(3): 191–207.

Mitra, S., & Quiroga, M. (2012). Children and the internet: A preliminary study in Uruguay. *International Journal of Humanities and Social Science 2*(15), 123–129. Retrieved from http://www.ijhssnet.com/journals/Vol_2_No_15_August_2012/15.pdf

Ofsted. (2012, December 11) *Innovative curriculum design to raise attainment: Middlestone Moor Primary School.* Reference No. 120372. Document now archived but available from https://nanopdf.com/download/middlestone-moor-primary-school_pdf

Pratham. (2019, May 19). *Wikipedia*. Retrieved from https://en.wikipedia.org/wiki/Pratham

Pratham India Education Initiative. (2009). *Pratham India Education Initiative: Annual report 2008–09*. Retrieved from http://pratham.org/file/Pratham Annual Report.pdf

Rothwell, J. (Director). (2018). *The school in the cloud* [Documentary film]. London, UK: Met Film Productions.

Roy, S. (2009, January 13). "Golden" diplomat basks in Slumdog glory. *The Indian Express*. Retrieved from https://indianexpress.com/article/cities/delhi/golden-diplomat-basks-in-slumdog-glory/

Skinner, B. F. (1964). New methods and new aims in teaching. *New Scientist, 122*. Retrieved online at https://www.bfskinner.org/publications/pdf-articles/

Stern, J., Ferraro, K., & Mohnkern, J. (2017). *Tools for teaching conceptual understanding, secondary: Designing lessons and assessments for deep learning*. Thousand Oaks, CA: Corwin.

Tyack, D., & Cuban, L. (1995). *Tinkering Toward Utopia: A century of public school reform*. Cambridge, MA: Harvard University Press.

Tyack, D., & Tobin, W. (1994). The "grammar" of schooling: Why has it been so hard to change?" *American Educational Research Journal, 31*(3), 453–479.

Tobin, L. (2009, March 2). Slumdog professor. *The Guardian*. Retrieved from https://www.theguardian.com/education/2009/mar/03/professor-sugata-mitra

Wackerbauer, R. (2010). *Complex dynamical systems*. Retrieved from the website of Dr. Renate Wackerbauer, University of Alaska Physics Department: http://ffden-2.phys.uaf.edu/wacker/

Wilby, P. (2016, June 7). Sugata Mitra—The professor with his head in the cloud. *The Guardian*. Retrieved from https://www.theguardian.com/education/2016/jun/07/sugata-mitra-professor-school-in-cloud

Wormeli, R. (2018, October). The problem with "Show Me the Research" thinking. *AMLE Magazine*. Retrieved from http://www.amle.org/BrowsebyTopic/WhatsNew/WNDet/TabId/270/ArtMID/888/ArticleID/963/The-Problem-with-Show-Me-the-Research-Thinking.aspx

INDEX

CORWIN

A SAGE Publishing Company

Helping educators make the greatest impact

CORWIN HAS ONE MISSION: to enhance education through intentional professional learning.

We build long-term relationships with our authors, educators, clients, and associations who partner with us to develop and continuously improve the best evidence-based practices that establish and support lifelong learning.

TMN195F7